The End of the Road Reader

THE END OF THE ROAD READER

Edited by
Karin Hokkanen and Anne Stewart

Northwoods Writers' Guild
Ely, MN

Copyright © 1997 by Northwoods Writers' Guild
All rights reserved including the right to reproduce this book by any means, electronic or mechanical, including photocopying or recording. All future rights to material published in this collection belong to the individual authors, and any reproduction or reprinting of this material may be done only with their permission.

Cover Woodcut by Becky Nosbisch

To order write
Northwoods Writers' Guild
c/o NLAA
P. O. Box 749
Ely, MN 55731-0749
35¢ per book sold goes to Northern Lakes Arts Association of Ely, Minnesota to help support the arts.

Printed by Echo Press, Alexandria, MN on recycled paper using soy ink

ISBN 1-886895-06-6

*To the memory of Charlotte Taylor Breaker,
a friend and a strong believer in all of us
who wanted to write.*

CONTENTS

Preface — i

Jane Whitledge	Morel Mushrooms	1
Bob Cary	The Voyageur	2
Robert Beymer	My Favorite Canoe Route	5
Becca Brin Manlove	An Otter at Supper Time	9
John David	The Ely Rock	11
Rose Thielbar	Mosquitoes	15
	The Jewel	17
Heart Warrior Chosa	Selections from her poetry	19
	Voice from the Boundary Waters (excerpted)	23
Cathy Dybiec Holm	The Green Cadillac	25
Farrell	Water	37
Anne Stewart	The Angler in the Green Hat	39
Pauline Steffy	Light Stepping	
	Two Birds	43
Margaret Sweet	The Velcro Cat	45
Robert Beymer	Destination Yet Unknown	47
	If Only We Could Be More Like the Chickadee	49
Louis Bernard	The Exploding Barrel Stove	51
	There Were Three	55

Barbara Murray	Legacy	59
	Woodcutter	61
Dawn DeWitt	Christmas Up North Where the Real Men Are	63
John David	Three Wise Moose	67
Becca Brin Manlove	Picnic	71
	Hauling Water	73
Karin Hokkanen	A Winter Memory	79
Margaret Sweet	I Remember	83
Lynn Rogers	The Orphaned Cubs	85
Anne Stewart	Envisioning a Landscape:	91
Robert Beymer	The Best and Worst of Times	99
Barbara Murray	Morning	101
	Desert Dreamtime	102
Heart Warrior Chosa	Irish Poems	103
Karin Hokkanen	Birch Time	105
Margaret Vos	Four Untitled Poems	107
Kaia DeShane	You Gave a Poem to Me	
	9 Mile Lake	109
	One That Rhymes	110
Jane Whitledge	Pussywillows	111
Contributors		113

Preface

During the fall of 1993, a few of us began discussing how nice it would be to get together on a regular basis to share work and to receive feedback and encouragement for whatever writing projects we were working on. We were given free use of the Ely Public Library conference room in the Community Center, and the Northwoods Writers' Guild began meeting twice a month. Members are an eclectic group of published and unpublished writers varying in styles and preferred wordsmith ways, all sharing a deep love of language and expression through the written word.

As we got to know each other over the weeks and months and our confidence grew, short stories, poems, essays, journal entries, and the beginnings of novels came to light. In February of 1995, the local radio station, WELY, allowed the writers' group some weekly air time to share original works with the public. Broadcasting was an opportunity to share unpublished thoughts and ideas, and as enthusiasm for reading on the air grew, several of us began to talk about putting our works together in published form. Summer residents and visitors often asked for locally written works at the local bookstore. We believed an open niche had presented itself, and we decided to fill it.

The process of collecting, reading, editing, and typesetting the manuscripts was done by the members of the Writers' Guild. Many of the selections in this book were first read aloud as part of our weekly broadcast on WELY Radio. WELY uses the phrase "at the end of the road" to describe itself, hence the name "The End of the Road Reader."

This anthology represents a slice of life from many angles. Each contribution reflects a lifestyle and love of the northwoods in an individual way according to the experience and outlook of the writer. Selections are arranged in accordance with the four well-defined seasons of the north country.

Thanks and appreciation go to our outside readers who gave feedback on the original manuscripts, to Patrick McKinnon at Poetry Harbor, Duluth, Minnesota, for invaluable assistance and counsel, and to the Northern Lakes Arts Association in Ely for administrative help. A big thank you to the Donald G. Gardner Trust for help with publishing costs.

We invite you to wander through the seasons with the writers showcased in this anthology. We hope you enjoy this unique perspective of our northern lifestyle and lake and woodland environment.

KH
Ely, MN
January, 1997

Imagination Tree   Karin A. Hokkanen

JANE WHITLEDGE

Morel Mushrooms

Softly they come
thumbing up from
firm ground

protruding unharmed.
Easily crumbled
and yet

how they shouldered
the leaf and mold
aside, rising

unperturbed
breathing obscurely,
still as stone.

By the slumping log,
by a dappled aspen,
they grow alone.

A dumb eloquence
seems their trade.
Like hooded monks

in a sacred wood
they say:
Tomorrow we are gone.

(first published in *Wilderness Magazine)*

Voyageur

Adventurer of waters north,
   With powered strokes your birchbark craft
Blazed trails where ancient tribes held forth
   And by their fires you sang and laughed.

A hundred years have passed-or more-
   Since last your paddles flashed the sun
On windswept waves by rockbound shore,
   Or in the spume of rapids run.

A hundred years...and yet in mist
   Of early dawn your song rings clear
Today...a chant that will persist
   Deep in the hearts of those who hear.

-Bob Cary
© 1981

ROBERT BEYMER

My Favorite Canoe Route

Over the past eighteen years, since publication of my first guide to the Boundary Waters Canoe Area, people have inquired about my favorite of all the canoeing routes through the wilderness. Until now, the answer was my secret.

My favorite canoeing route begins with a long drive on a winding, narrow forest road through the heart of Superior National Forest. The primitive gravel road ends at a small parking lot, just large enough for three or four automobiles. The lot is seldom occupied and never full. I'm not worried about sharing "my route" with other people. Only one overnight group is allowed to explore the wilderness each day from this peaceful access.

From the north end of that small parking lot a foot trail gradually descends through a lovely forest of jackpines to the base of a rapids. The path is narrow but quite smooth considering the small amount of regular foot traffic to wear down the path.

The river at that point is not as wide as my canoe is long. Banks are choked with alder. Sandbars require wide swings around tight corners, a feat best accomplished in a canoe no longer than sixteen feet. Occasionally, the tiny river is barricaded by twigs and branches, the result of ambitious beavers working through the previous night, only to be broken each day by canoes like mine.

Most of the first day of this route is on the river with an ideal combination of paddling and portaging. In just minutes I am immersed in wilderness. No other people. No sights or sound of human intrusion, except my own. Several short portages bypass sets of rapids that are strewn with too many boulders to permit the safe running, lining or walking of a canoe on the river. Each portage is long enough to stretch my back and legs, to invigorate my heart and lungs, but short enough to avoid serious fatigue and muscle strain. Each meandering river segment between portages is long enough to exercise my arms and shoulders while not so long as to render them weary from paddling.

The final portage leads to a small lake with a lovely campsite on its north shore. A gentle breeze holds mosquitoes at bay. The fire grate sits on a granite outcropping that affords a view of both the setting sun and the rising moon. The ancient rock is terraced. The highest level provides a flat, smooth surface on which to sleep, with just enough glacial soil to separate the hard, cool granite from the floor of my self-supporting tent. A lower level projects onto a small point and serves nicely as a "dining room" with seats resting against the vertical shelf that holds the "kitchen" just above. The lowest visible terrace provides a shelf at the water's edge, at a perfect height to scoop up water for cooking and cleaning. Yet another flat rock shelf rests a couple feet below the water's surface, ideal for safely launching warm bodies into the cool lake.

On the second day of my favorite route, a chain of small lakes leads deeper into the wilderness. Portages are longer and more challenging than those crossed the previous day. One trail is nearly a mile long, climbs steeply near the middle and then dips through a low, muddy bog. Most wilderness visitors avoid it. It's the price one must pay for ultimate solitude.

I find small lakes, rivers, and creeks much more desirable, under normal circumstances, than large lakes. Strong winds that often whip up dangerously high waves and whitecaps on "big water" are rarely a concern on the smaller, more protected lakes and streams. The intimacy with Nature that one feels on tiny lakes and narrow creeks is an even more compelling reason to seek them out. When both shorelines are clearly visible from a silent canoe, playful mink darting in and out of crevasses on the rocky bank are not overlooked. Nor are the painted turtles sunning themselves on logs resting in shallow water. A spotted fawn standing motionless in tall grass and reeds would surely be missed by paddlers in the middle of a large lake. For that matter, so would a large bull moose standing majestically behind a clump of shrubbery at the water's edge. None of Nature's family is likely to be overlooked from the vantage point of a quiet canoe on a tiny lake or stream.

Lunch is served on a small, barren island with no trees and only a few shrubs growing from cracks in huge boulders. Warm sunshine relaxes tightness in my neck and shoulders. Nothing could taste better than a peanut butter and jelly sandwich!

My campsite this night rests in a distant corner of a medium-sized lake far from the two portage trails leading to and from the lake. The site is high on a small peninsula facing a large bog on the opposite shoreline. As the orange sun drops behind the forested horizon of black spruce and balsam fir, a large cow moose and two calves slowly emerge onto the edge of the bog. I watch quietly until the scene succumbs to darkness.

A decision must be made on the morning of the third day. Every good route plan includes options to consider along the way. At this point I could veer northwest on a loop that would take three more full days to complete. Or I could enjoy a layover day here and then travel two more days toward the southwest.

This time I choose the latter alternative. Laying over at this campsite affords an opportunity to explore a seldom-used hiking trail that loops through the heart of the Boundary Waters. Walking without canoe and pack is a delightful change of pace. The lakes and woods are seen from unique perspectives not enjoyed by paddlers.

Dense forests of aspen and birch, spruce and tamarack, red and white pines yield to occasional clearings of low cattail swamps or high, bald ridges. When the trail skirts the edge of a vertical cliff, the scenic view across several small lakes is spectacular.

The last half of my favorite route is more difficult than the first. By now toned muscles are accustomed to the physical strain of paddling and portaging. Campsite chores are routine. Longer, steeper portages are welcomed as a challenge. Paddling one day on large lakes is a pleasant change. Although stronger winds often sweep across the surface of a large lake, there is always that slim chance that calm will prevail. Few wilderness experiences are more inspirational than gliding across a vast expanse of ripple-free water. Engulfed by a perfect reflection of clouds and sky, you could be floating through heaven itself.

My favorite trip concludes on another small, winding stream that leads to another lightly used entry point within walking distance to my point of origin.

Though not found on any one particular map, routes like this are found on numerous maps of the Quetico-Superior canoe country. Entry points that see few visitors, winding rivers and small lakes, at least one rugged portage to separate the serious expeditioner from the casual camper, campsites on granite outcrops, a layover hike, and all the rest combine to create an ideal route for anyone who seeks a truly memorable journey through the world's most unique canoeing wilderness.

An Otter at Suppertime

V's of light
on the evening-calm
lake announced
her coming.
We scooped our suppers
onto tin plates,
settled into niches
on the steep granite slope,
heels holding us in place,
our thighs our tables.
At the narrow place
below us she dove.
We waited, forks poised;
a desperate splash,
the bass in the otter's mouth writhed,
its tail sprayed water
in shimmering arcs
above the otter's head.
She swam to the opposite shore,
hunched and slid her dripping length
onto a low, rock shelf.
We ate our suppers
to the crunching of fish bones.
She ate hers
to the clicking of forks on tin.

JOHN DAVID

The Ely Rock

Dear Bobo,

It's time for my monthly letter from Ely, and the subject this time is the Ely Rock. Now, before you throw my effort in the trash, just take a minute and read on, because what I have written will delight and amaze you.

I first became aware of The Rock about two years ago while having dinner in a local restaurant. My place mat turned out to be an Ely town map that highlighted all kinds of spiffy things to see and do. Item #14, down in the lower left corner, was the Ely Rock, located just a stone's throw from the veterinary clinic. According to the place mat, The Rock was 2.7 billion years old! Wow! Just imagine! That thing had been sitting around in the twelve hundred block of Main Street for almost three billion years! This I had to see for myself.

As soon as I finished my creamed chipped beef, I hopped in my truck and beat it over to Main Street. Sure enough, right by the side of the road was this monster rock, about ten feet tall and fifteen feet wide at the base. Affixed to the rock was a sign that states the following:

> Pillow Rock. Ely Greenstone Outcrop.
> Rare Ellipsoidal lava flow formed beneath
> primal seas 2.7 billion years ago.

You know, Bobo, the longer I live in this town the more I love it. Imagine. A rock. Right here in Ely, Minnesota, 2.7 billion years old. We sure didn't have anything like that back in Baltimore.

This past weekend I had some visitors, a couple that I hadn't seen in years. I remembered that in college he had majored in geology, so I was positive that he was going to like visiting the Ely Rock. I figured she would like it, too, because she always concurred in his opinions; that's how they got along for all these years.

When they arrived I gave them the grand tour; everything in this town worth seeing. Right after I showed them the Dairy Queen, I took them to see the rock, because as the crow flies, the two are pretty close.

Just as I thought, he loved it. But surprisingly, she was skeptical and started to ask hostile questions:

"Who said it was 2.7 billion years old?" she demanded of me.

"Old Man Mose," I replied.

Her eyes narrowed, and she looked at me real hard. "Well. How did he know?"

I stared right back at her. "Somebody left him a note."

She was having a hard time with all of this. "How come there's a chain link fence around it?"

She almost had me on that one. But I had done my homework and was ready for anything. When I first saw the Ely Rock, I, too, noticed the chain link fence. I assumed it was there to protect the rock from midnight scalawags. You know the type. They sneak around in the dark with cans of spray paint, bent upon desecrating our treasured monuments with graffiti. In the dark they write awful things, like "Nancy Loves the Cheese Man" or, even worse, stuff like "The Class of '23 Will Live Forever!"

But I was wrong. Boy was I wrong. In an unguarded moment, one of the locals told me that Ely, like Peyton Place, had a little secret. Apparently, some fifteen years ago, a fellow from Iowa was visiting Ely with his wife, their two kids, and their little dog Fluffy. While this family was observing the Ely Rock, it suddenly lurched forward and ran over the poor man's left foot. His shoe was completely ruined, not to mention all of his foot bones. People dismissed the event as a freak accident; perhaps the rock had been dislodged by an earthquake or something like that.

But two years later an even worse event happened. A

tour group showed up; a bunch of ladies, each of whom had won first prize in her respective division for selling great quantities of Tupperware. In recognition of a job well done, they had all won an expense-paid trip to our fair city.

The tour bus fetched them from place to place, and eventually they descended upon the Ely Rock. While the ladies were assembled about the rock, each lost in her private thoughts, it suddenly rolled forward completely squishing a woman who had produced two thousand seven hundred fourteen dollars in sales volume. It was horrible, Bobo. First a foot, then a whole person. The Ely Rock was beginning to act like a killer tomato, rolling over people without provocation. If the word got out, you could kiss our tourist revenues goodbye. No one was going to visit a rock with an attitude, even if it was just behind the Dairy Queen.

Into the chaos that followed stepped our city fathers. For three days and nights they debated the issues behind the locked doors of City Hall. When at last they stepped out into the sunlight, they had formulated a perfect solution: the rock would be surrounded by a chain link fence.

As an idea it was a tour de force. To the innocent tourist, it would appear that the fence was to protect the rock. But in truth, the fence was there to restrain the rock and thus protect the tourists from any unpleasantness.

And that's exactly what happened. In all the years since the fence was placed around the rock, not one tourist has been lost. The rock has been held in check, securely anchored in place and rendered harmless.

I love this town, Bobo. I love our rock. But most of all I love our city fathers, who give real meaning to your favorite word, "perspicacious."

My friend's wife was still waiting for an answer. As a member of this community I had an obligation to contribute, to help the town grow and prosper. And if necessary, to protect the tourist revenues, I had an obligation to keep our dark secret from the rest of the world.

So I looked her right in the eye and lied.

"The fence is there so that naughty people won't vandalize our rock."

She accepted my explanation, and I felt warm and fuzzy for the rest of the day.

Well, Bobo, that's all for now. The topic of next month's letter will be "The Polka, As An Enduring Art Form."

Your Pal,

John

ROSE THIELBAR

Mosquitoes 1995

"Twas early October
down at the dock.
The morning was warm, so I
paused from my walk.
Never was summer so
scorchingly dry.
Wildfire smoke lingered
for months in the sky.

But something was good
about this dry year
Fewer mosquitoes were
buzzing my ear.
Believe it or not,
some days there weren't any!
When it comes to mosquitoes
not any is plenty.

We had a good freeze
to knock those pests out.
But here was a new swarm
flying about.
Thing that's peculiar
about this late batch,
They're so feeble and frail
their eggs may not hatch.

Can you believe it?
Mosquitoes this small?
Too weak to lay eggs and
just hatched this fall.
Dare I to dream it?

Hey, what do you think?
By nineteen ninety-six
mosquitoes extinct?

Then should we be worried
about our feathered friends?
It's no laughing matter if
a whole species ends.
What will birds eat if
each mosquito dies?
I don't see a problem.
Let them eat black flies.

ROSE THIELBAR

The Jewel

In my hand I held a jewel: precious, shining, emerald-green. The underside was white like marble with a patch of obsidian black. It was so delicate that I held it gently and lightly, hardly daring to touch it at all. The black patch was changeable and had a glow that seemed to come from within. It would radiate colors from black to iridescent orange to brilliant ruby red.

Just before I picked up this fallen gem, a humming sound came from it, and it was like a dancing, shimmering rainbow, all light and color and motion. It darted from flower to flower in my garden, dashing right and left, backwards, and sometimes in a pendulum arc. On each side of this tiny gem were fragile gossamer wings which could be extended or folded back. But one wing wasn't folded back quite like its twin. Ah, this then was its flaw.

I held this precious substance in my hand trying to will some warmth and strength back into it. The light was growing fainter, and I was powerless to keep the light burning. And when, too soon, the light went out of this living jewel, sadness flowed out from my eyes in streams of tears.

DREAM LODGE POEMS

by Heart Warrior Chosa

HEART WARRIOR CHOSA
(excerpts from Dream Lodge Poems)

Do not perceive me as a creative writer belonging to a writer's world, but rather as a scout, as in days gone by.
  I am the one who rides ahead, has read the tracks, and reports what I've seen—the course of action and the reasons. I report to twin councils, one of earth and one of nonearth; both councils of power

     Ho! Coming prancing
        Coming prancing
           Coming prancing
              Coming prancing and singing.

With fleet swiftness of a young stallion chasing the springtime dawn of red robed people.

———

Pierce my soul...
    my heart...
neighing fluted speech
of a black stallion.

Rushing air elementals
streaking my windy mane.

Free nocturnal nomad.
The full red moon
a crown upon his head.

———

THUNDER QUEEN
> Ten times twenty-two
> in the life you hold.

THUNDER QUEEN
> Bring down walls as only you can
> and whisper to me all the things
> unheard of.

THUNDER QUEEN
> Because you know why
> and in all your learning teach

WARRIOR MOTHER IS MY NAME
> I am beyond a Queen.
> In my army are a million Amazons
> Our colors are red and white.
>
> My battlefield, friends and foes—
> are earthen vials.
>
> Smitten are those under my ethereal sword.
> Nurtured are those in the molten lava of my
>   heart.
> Protected by my mother's bosom.
>
> The owl whispers my name before the dawn
> portends the unveiling of the sun.

IN THE WIND
There's a red horse on the red earth running freely in
The red heart of Mother Earth.

White clay cleaves to her hooves like
your image to my mind.

I go now into the wilderness cradle
to be rocked by my mother.
Where companions cannot go.
Where Indians dream alone.

On the hill of inspiration
In the pit of aspiration.
Where waters give up their secrets
moving with great speed.

Slowly, cautiously
aware of my puniness.
Searching for something,
Somewhere I die.

What kind of death
I do not know.

In the middle of the hurricanes mighty
force is utter stillness.
And there in the valley of utopia grew the most exquisite flower......in the sky an electric breeze of the South Winds blew permeated by its exotic perfume.....in spiraled circles sought to lightly, lightly caress, embrace and bathe as one.
So intimate, and gentle close, so far away.
The magnetism of a flower
captures the eye of a tornado.

excerpt from
Five Pointed Star Consciousness

Bowing down on my knees at
the crossroads I remember.
Black Elk said this place was
holy and the center of the universe.

Ho! What's this? Kali dancing
and gnashing duality in her teeth!
A black Ah Kii, sacred spirit;
trampling down those who defile
her creations

She rattles the skulls made
into a necklace about her throat.
"make SOUND to create your reality,"
said she. AH.

On her forehead is the golden
catseye, from the first world;
the eye of an eagle. "FOCUS INTENT,"
and, "go on winged Bear Power," she
intoned. OM.

"Let the thread of your heart be
FREE, PURE, AND ONE with All threaded
STAR patterns. Link life to
Life." Compassion. HUM

Whirling I dance Life; like an
Indian princess at the pow wow, in
a Gypsy wind. A circle within a circle,
radiating to infinity—never finding
the "ring pass not," because I am
always HOME.

HEART WARRIOR CHOSA

excerpt from
Voice from the Boundary Waters Canoe Area

My lake, home of my father's people, land from whence the substance of my body came,... generations echo through the hallways of my veins and beat my little drum between the ribs making songs that delight....You, I claim as kin,....The soft lap of water on rock tells secrets of your lineage as the turtles on warm June nights pound the sand beach to empty life.

My lake, in how many lifetimes have you drawn me to your shore, and enchantress and coolest lover....you were always faithful. In...clean shadows and little nests creatures have peace from "manifest destiny." Black bears sit along a bank in the last rays of the setting sun and loons enchant the sleep and in song punctuate the right moment—I light the sacred pipe, breath of life. Sometimes in dancing...crystalline water foam, in the violet shadows of...sun soaked days, you'll see the eagle catch his prey.
....

My lake, my mother's shielding arms; who...seeks to steal you from me? Who is this...gold hunter...?....What kind of blindness is it that does not see your sacredness?....We know your body houses all that is sacred. Speak, whisper holy words that I might understand. You are invincible, it is known.

Time to get up, move with the dawn before little birds...moving silently toward the sweat lodge....Stoke the sacred four directions fire, purify, leaving secret messages. Such peaceful tranquility exists no where else....

My lake, my path in life. Hey, grandfather tree, tell me what you saw. Grandfather trees are almost all gone....

That four mile portage path is lined with great moose tracks and little green worms the ants drag away. They must taste sweet because ants need honey for their queen in springtime. I must remember to bring them honey so they will bring the rain.

The Thunderers are absent this spring. My mother, she was Thunder Being clan, and so I am their special chick and will surely sing the welcome song when they come visiting.

My relatives are growing less; the atmosphere can no longer hold them, and they dissipate....

My lake, much loved lake, they are here for you; they want your gold, copper, nickel, platinum, uranium....But first they want the tree nation; ...home to thousands of wingeds, attractors of rain, givers of oxygen, holders of earthen soil who will feed the sun this summer.

My lake, how well you speak, my dearest friend....you say it won't be so....won't it be a surprise when...your great body moves and deep red caverns open lava doors where molten hot liquid beats rhythm with your soul.

My lake, when you break free could it be the heart of a great Turtle breaking and will my heart break with yours to join the sun, or will I be an old woman to teach the children and recall for them how it used to be?

CATHY DYBIEC HOLM

The Green Cadillac with the Creamy Leather Seats

"Look for the green Cadillac, the one with the creamy leather seats," Phil muttered sleepily as he slumped on the couch in the corner of the gas station lounge.

It was 6:30 a.m., on Thursday, and the men of Turtle River were gathered at the town gas station to discuss politics, to gossip, and to expound on the woes of the world. Freshly made coffee steamed in a stained metal percolator, smelling hot and bitter. Granules of sugar and nondairy creamer adorned the tablecloth interspersed with month-old coffee stains. The heavy smell of cigar smoke clashed fiercely with a stale cigarette odor.

"Who the hell would drive a car like that around here anyway?" grumbled Omar, owner of the station. Omar's stomach jutted belligerently over his belt and threatened to burst the seams of his red, white, and blue American flag shirt. His small eyes craftily surveyed the room and his buddies, making sure that no one was putting something past him.

Roger filled his stained mug with the bitter brew. "Well,...I don't think she's from around here. I've never seen her before, and she doesn't look like she's related to anyone." A tall man with a round, face, Roger went through life easily, and talked the same way.

"Ain't nobody around here who's got the money to drive a car like that," grunted Omar. "Got to be a tourist."

"Well all I know," mumbled Phil through hung-over fog, "is that she drove in here yesterday, paid for gas with a platinum American Express card—I mean how often do you see those?—and asked about some place for writers called Coffee Haven. Ever heard of it?" Phil had aspirations to write a best selling novel but didn't dare tell these guys—fearing they'd spread the word all over town.

"Well Phil, why didn't ya ask her?" grinned Omar evilly. "Notice if she was married? You coulda had a nice sugar mama."

"Yeah, you coulda been a kept man," slurped Banty, easily the most extroverted of the bunch and already on his fourth cup of coffee. "Well guys, gotta run. Got places to go, houses to sell, suckers to con...ha, ha—just kidding, Roger."

"Up yours," muttered Roger amiably, slapping Banty on the back as the realtor hurried out the metal door.

The men moved on to a heated discussion of topics ranging from the Bosnian War to the appearance of a second hardware store in Turtle River. Phil, normally an active part of these conversations, daydreamed about writing poetry and fiction. Who was this woman who had sailed through town in her green Cadillac, blithely flashing high class plastic and asking about Coffee Haven? She mentioned a weekend writing class in Pela. His curiosity peaked—someone around town ought to know who she was and where she was staying. He would find a way to meet her.

***

Maura brushed her thick, black hair out of her eyes and distractedly veered the green Cadillac onto an endless dirt road. Any road would do...she needed time to digest the events of the past few weeks. She had some time to kill until Friday. She worked her way to Pela with the directions given from the guy at the Turtle River Gas Station.

After checking into a Pela hotel, she decided to explore the country. Accelerating, the car hurtled through the spruce lined road at 85 MPH.

"What kind of slob would leave week-old dried dog

crap all over my house because he was too lazy to clean it up?" she fumed internally. Maura referred to her husband Dale, who was back in St. Paul now, probably pacing the house and wondering where she had gone. Well, screw him. Let him wonder. After all, any man who was inconsiderate enough to not clean up dog shit while she worked didn't deserve to be worried about.

Maura had snapped two days ago when Dale began teasing her about her home-based word processing business. "Click! Click!" he repeated endlessly and monotonously, imitating the sound of her fingers tapping on the keyboard and brainwashing the kids to join his obnoxious chorus. "Click! Click!" they smugly sang in unison.

"Passive-aggressive son-of-a-bitch," Maura screamed, hurling the nearest heavy object, a stapler, at Dale's face. Dale showed uncharacteristic savvy and ducked just in time. But Maura had enough. She grabbed an overnight bag, stuffed it with a few changes of clothes and necessary toiletries, and peeled out of the driveway leaving burned tire rubber and exhaust as a parting souvenir.

"Head for the woods. Head for the woods," a little voice nagged, piquing Maura's long neglected intuition. She had no idea why, but she raced toward the interstate, zoomed onto the entrance ramp, and aimed the car toward northern Minnesota. The lure of the wild beckoned; the trees looked greener, thicker, and more inviting than an arboretum. She was suddenly more aware of the sky than she had ever been. It loomed close and searing, larger than life. The heavy traffic seemed to fall off the sides of the earth as the Cadillac put distance between itself and the busy cities.

"Jesus, Get me out of this hell-hole," she seethed, thinking about her demanding family and her incompetent husband. "I'm taking a trip and I can do whatever I want —it's my time—only my time." Savagely she twisted the radio dial from the kid's favorite rap station to Minnesota Public Radio. A Chopin prelude floated from the speakers and Maura sank into the Cadillac's soft leather seats and began to relax. Aimlessly she turned over in her head the many, suddenly obvious instances of Dale's attempts to sabotage her career. He was a jerk all right. It'd be nice to put some space between them for a few days. I'm not even going to miss him, she realized.

Hypnotized by the freeway scenery, she almost missed the announcement following the music. "We want to let aspiring Minnesota writers know that we're holding our annual writing retreat at Coffee Haven in Pela, Minnesota," an earnest, cultured, young male voice read. "This includes writers of fiction, nonfiction, and poetry. We're located on First Street near Northstar Avenue. Cost is minimal and the retreat runs this Friday through Sunday. We hope that you'll join us."

Images of fellow writers comparing notes and sharing stories wafted through Maura's head. She visualized penning stories in the quiet northern woods, housed in a small rustic cabin with wind sifting through the pines and soothing urban writers' tired ears. Impulsively, she knew that Pela had to be her destination. Mentally she charted out the best way to get there.

***

On Thursday afternoon, after his morning gas station shift, Phil began a personal crusade to find out about the mysterious Cadillac that had driven into his life. He stopped first at the office of the *Turtle River News*, source of all printable and unprintable nuggets regarding local happenings. Ada, a skinny vulture of a woman with cats-eye glasses and an unerring instinct for good gossip, cornered Phil as he walked in the door.

"What do you know, Phil? Anything new?" Her sharp eyes snapped furiously and expectantly. Ada felt the world owed her juicy news, and wasn't ashamed to show it.

"Actually," Phil brushed his hair from his sleepy face, "I was hoping you could give me some information. Do you know anything about a woman who cruised through here on Wednesday in a fancy green Cadillac?"

"What's the matter, Phil, aren't you going out with that cute little Wendy anymore?" Ada probed, preferring to wrap up a good story rather than chasing down information that might not be worth the effort.

"Aw...Wendy and I are ancient history," Phil's blue eyes seemed to mist for a minute and then hardened into glinting diamonds, realizing that he'd given Ada yet another piece of news. "But seriously, what do you know about this woman—anything?"

"I wish I did," Ada hated to admit that she didn't have a handle on every happening in Turtle River, "but I haven't heard a thing. I'll give you a call if I find out anything—ok?"

"Yeah, right...well, I'll see ya." Phil knew that Ada would probably be busy digging up juicier stories unless the green Cadillac turned into a hot item. He closed the door on the sounds of newspaper production and headed down the street into the sunlight.

Early Friday morning, Phil headed toward Pela in his dented, black, Ford pickup. He'd managed to hit the road at 6 a.m. so he'd be long gone when the guys at the station noticed him missing at the morning coffee session. Adorned proudly with a rear bumper sticker "My Baby Is American-Made," the truck rattled through the backwoods roads and shook Phil into a wide-awake stupor. Phil was a night person and fought waking every inch of the way.

Sleepily, Phil reminisced about his last visit to Pela ten years ago. For some reason, he just never seemed to make it over that way, even though it sat only fifty miles to the east of Turtle River. He recalled a nondescript town with the usual cafe, bar, and a few stores, including the Guns and Roses Pawnshop.

A half hour later, Phil rounded a sharp turn in the two lane road and found himself on the Pela main drag. Immediately he could see the town had changed. Tired, decrepit bars had been replaced with cutesy, northwoods paraphernalia shops. There were more people on the streets than he remembered, even at 7 a.m. Groups of tourists (they had to be tourists with their flashy clothes and shiny cars that had never seen a dirt road) congregated with surprising alertness and headed down the road for blueberry pancakes at Merle's Eating Establishment.

Feeling a mixture of panic and disgust, Phil almost turned around. These well dressed yuppies and the new flavor of the town made him uncomfortable for reasons he couldn't put his finger on. Resolving to learn about writing he headed farther down the street and located Coffee Haven.

***

Coffee Haven sat on a street one block from the Pela main drag looking like a hometown bar poorly disguised as a coffeehouse. The place had been rescued from destruction by its 90's-hippie owners, Rena and Sax. "Hell no, we won't go!" a sign happily announced on the doorway. The owners refused to shop at franchised grocery stores preferring to frequent farmers' markets and the rare co-op.

Rena padded around the kitchen in sandals and a long sundress, readying dozens of coffeepots for the avid writers that she knew would show up. This was the fourth annual Coffee Haven Writers' Retreat; she still vividly remembered the collective energy of old and new writers as they struggled to put their unique voices onto paper. Of course, lots of strong coffee and homemade muffins helped the creative process.

Rena was an armchair artist; she enjoyed watching the creative process at work even though she practiced no art herself.

"Come on in," she yelled, noticing Phil rapping at the front door. "Are you here for the writers' retreat?"

"Yeah, I guess," Phil mumbled diffidently. It felt strange to admit out loud that he thought of himself as a writer.

"Sax, get those muffins out of the oven. Have a seat. Here's some coffee." Rena bustled about the place in a sudden flurry of activity. Phil sat down at the nearest round table and scanned the Pela newspaper, a less gossipy version of the *Turtle River News*. He forgot his uneasiness and relaxed in the unpretentiousness of Coffee Haven.

***

By the time Maura located Coffee Haven and edged the Cadillac carefully into a street parking spot, it was late on Friday morning, and the Writers' Retreat was three hours into the program. Writers sat gathered in small working groups as a portly, bearded fellow named Dylan facilitated from the front of the room. An aura of academia and self-importance emanated from Dylan; the writers acted appropriately and treated him with deference and a little awe. Dylan's frizzy hair perfectly complimented his baggy pants, tie-dye smock, and huaraches.

Maura glanced around the room and took the last available spot at a table near the front. Her fellow writers sat gripping their pens and stared hard at empty notebooks in deep concentration. Some of the students smiled tentatively at her. Good, she thought, this seems like a friendly bunch. Rena swung by quickly to collect the session fee and give Maura some writing materials and a fresh cup of coffee. Dylan stared at the wall, deep in thought with his chin planted firmly on his hand. He seemed to be gathering his strength for some future event.

"Now," Dylan, straightened up suddenly and faced the audience, "we have spent time this morning learning to simplify our sentences..." He paused to glare at one guilty writer in the corner of the room and then continued, "and to add excitement and description to our writing. We are each going to try to pinpoint what we want to write about in the remainder of our time together."

"What," Dylan's grey eyes suddenly snapped and focused in on Maura, "do **you** think you want to write about?"

Straight from the gut her answer came after temporarily recoiling from Dylan's sudden focus.

"I want to write about the blues," Maura blurted. The words were out of her mouth before she knew what she'd said.

"The **blues?** You? Excuse me, but I don't think you'd know the blues if they hit you in the face," Dylan said, with more than a hint of arrogance. "Nobody wants to read about white-girl-middle-class blues."

"More like upper-class-white girl......did you see the car she drove up in?" softly muttered a catty participant to his companion.

"Excuse me!" Maura was indignant. Her face plainly showed emotions from vulnerability to rage. This was quickly turning into the Writers' Retreat from Hell. How dare this arrogant man ruin her first chance at freedom; her chance to do what she wanted. Her heart pounded, and her skin flushed with hot excitement. "How do you know what I can and can't write about?" Maura held her ground. "How do you even know I'm white?"

"Lady," Dylan mouthed the words haughtily, "it's written all over your face. You must write what you know, and, personally, I'd be real surprised if you could muster up any two tone blues for me today."

"Of, fuck you." Maura grabbed her notebook and slammed the door hard on the way out. Dylan seemed unsure of what to do next. The writers fidgeted uncomfortably in their seats. Rena swung around the kitchen door and, unsettled by the new mood in the room, abruptly dropped a large tray of blueberry muffins all over the floor.

"Well folks," began Dylan, a little less securely, "how about we each generate a page's worth of what we want to write about, and then compare notes." The room gradually fell silent except for the etching of pencils on lined, white paper.

***

Banty readied his real estate float for the Friday afternoon Annual Boat Parade. No fancy float this—his old pickup truck with the "Northern Swamp Realty" sign on the side would do. Heck, there was even a hole where there used to be a sunroof. Banty would make sure that his smiling face was inscribed in the memory of every Turtle River parade spectator. Maybe he could snag a few of these rich tourists that continued to invade the area and buy luxurious lake homes. A few more commissions and he might even be able to take the rest of the summer off and do some fishing. Or better yet, invest some time and get Banty's Bait Business off the ground.

The Annual Boat Parade was a ten-year-old tradition in town designed to draw tourists and locals alike. People drove and walked all manner of things to be part of this parade, but a prize was given for the fanciest boat in the lineup. Usually a tourist walked away with the booty, but last year Omar had snatched the prize by finding a trailer big enough to haul his houseboat down the main drag. At 6:30 a.m., for the next month at Union 76 Omar had relived his day of glory.

***

Unsteadily Maura headed back to Turtle River. That arrogant Dylan had really tried to burst her bubble. Maura was sorry she'd ever gone to the writers' retreat. She'd hoped she'd emerge with a clear sense of the quality and direction of her writing. Now she felt rudderless and more confused than before.

Angrily she recalled the morning's events. Why couldn't she write about the blues? She knew as much about the bad times as anyone. "I bet that uppity Dylan had life handed to him on a silver spoon," she grumbled.

Seething with frustration and anxiety, Maura wondered what it would feel like to go insane and had a feeling that she was pretty darned close. The Cadillac careened crazily down the two lane highway, but Maura paid only minimal attention to driving. She hardly noticed the approaching Turtle River Gift Shop.

"I dare you," she muttered intensely to an imaginary writing instructor. "I dare you to tell me about the blues! Needlenosed, academic nerd." She could picture Dylan in her head preaching dry, overused cliches about writing. "Write what you know," he intoned endlessly. She raged, thinking about the men in her life who got great joy out of putting her down.

Vaguely she became aware of people lining the streets. Where had they come from? They stood in groups, staring at the pavement expectantly. What were they waiting for?

A frizzy haired man in the crowd looked vaguely familiar. Maura sharply veered the Cadillac toward the sidewalk to get a better look.

"Dylan," she screamed, forgetting that she'd just left Dylan an hour ago, "You jerk!" The Cadillac windows rolled down like smooth, oiled machinery. Amazed spectators jumped back from the curb, fearing for their safety.

Maura leaned over the passenger seat barely steering

the car away from the curious and startled onlookers. "Tell me about the blues," she yelled at the amazed man. "I dare you. I want to know. Tell me what you know about bad times—I mean really bad times. I bet you could fit what you know into a thimble. I bet you could fit your brain into a thimble."

"What the hell are you talking about?" the amazed man shouted, but Maura careened down the remainder of Main Street before she could see that the man looked nothing like Dylan. Burning rubber, she sped out of town and never noticed the parade that was getting started behind her.

***

"Well," muttered Ada to herself, "I guess I'll pay more attention the next time Phil comes in here with some news." In her mind she replayed the day's events. That green Cadillac had come back to town after all, only to raise a ruckus during the parade and nearly run over Banty's brother from out of town. When Ada questioned spectators they came forth with splotchy information about a crazy woman hollering something about the blues from her fancy car. Well, it'd make good copy for the *Turtle River News*—she'd been having a hard time coming up with lively stories lately. She could guarantee that every subscriber would be waiting eagerly for the next issue.

***

"Holy shit, I guess we're losing our touch, boys." The Union 76 gang was slowly waking up to the start of another day. Three of the guys in the room had had high hopes of winning the float prize yesterday only to be upstaged by the crazy woman in that Cadillac. Banty was particularly peeved. No one had noticed much of anything, including his Northern Swamp Realty truck after the Cadillac incident.

"Hey, where the hell's Phil been?" muttered Roger. "I haven't seen him for a couple days now."

"Who knows. Chasing after the big green Cadillac in the sky, I guess," Omar sneered. "He always had his head up his ass."

"Say guys, have I got a deal for you." Banty's wheels were spinning, never one to be too long offset by the unexpected. "See, I'm trying to get Banty's Bait Business started, and I need some leeches. Now I know that at least two of you here have ponds on your property. If you let me take what I need, I'll give you five percent of the cut. Whadaya say?"

Another day began to unfold in Turtle River.

***

FARRELL

Water

water
water
i
water
beg you
water
please
water
i need
water
water
water
bless you
water
thank
water
you
water
that's
water
enough
water
not so
water
fast
water
please
water
no
water
more
water
wat
water
i
water

Dinnertime   Karin A. Hokkanen

ANNE STEWART

The Angler in the Green Hat

Lynn Beck felt satisfaction as he watched a boat slow and its occupant ease the boat into position over the reef where Lynn was fishing. "This farmer looks like he knows what he's doing," Lynn told himself. "If he's fishing this close to me, it must mean the walleye are here." Lake Angelina was known for its big walleye.

The man in the other boat switched off the motor and dropped anchor. He wore jeans, a short-sleeved, plaid shirt, and a bright-green cap with the name of a seed company stitched above the bill. The man's moves were slow, thoughtful as he carefully put a worm on a hook.

Lynn was jigging with a minnow on the bottom, the best way, he had been told, to catch walleye. He wasn't having any success. Sitting in his downtown office several weeks ago, Lynn had remembered fishing with his father, once. He suddenly had an urge to return to nature, be an outdoorsman. He had gone to Gander Mountain, bought clothing and equipment, taken a week off, and come north to fish.

Lynn watched the man in the other boat let out line down through the water. A gust of wind came skipping across the lake and swung both boats on their anchor ropes. At the same time, Lynn's rod bent. He pulled and the line held fast, no give at all. "Damn rocks," he muttered to himself. He played the line as if he had a fish. He felt like a fool, getting caught in the rocks. He was sure the other guy was laughing at him.

Without pulling up the anchor, Lynn maneuvered the boat to another angle to try and loosen his line. He kept his back to the other boat. With some tugging and pulling, he managed to free his line. He then gave a mighty jerk and swore, to make it look as if he had lost a fish.

The other man watched Lynn play and loose the imaginary fish. The way the rod had bent over it seemed like a good fish.

An hour passed with no action in either boat. Lynn saw the other man reel in and add a jig to the worm, and let the line back out and down to the bottom of the lake.

Lynn felt the other man's gaze on him. Lynn was dressed in light-weight, olive-green, outdoor wear: Patagonia pants, loose fitting cotton shirt, olive-green life vest, and an olive-green, cotton canvas hat. He had lures fastened to his hat. He had tried to look like one of the fishing pros on TV.

"Nice day, Lynn said to the man." The man grunted affirmation.

Lynn had been on the water since 5 o'clock that morning. Now he gave in to the pangs of hunger, pulled the minnow basket from the water, and put it into the bucket, and pulled up the anchor. He moved so no one could see if he brought a stringer of fish into the boat or not. Lynn gave an unconscious pull to his olive-green hat to make it firm on his head, started the motor, and sped down the lake, fishing lures flapping on his hat.

Lynn did not go back out until after lunch. On his way to his boat he passed the fish cleaning house and saw a barrel full of walleye guts and heads and thought, "I'll bet that farmer in the green hat cleaned up after I came in."

Lynn saw Tom Yanich, sitting in a boat tied to the dock, sorting fishing tackle. He looked at ease. "A local," Lynn thought.

Yanich was a fishing guide, and he and his clients had had a successful morning.

"Did a guy in a green hat catch a lot of fish today?" Lynn asked the guide. Lynn put on his own olive-green hat.

Tom looked up from his tackle box. He considered the question; then an easy smile spread across his face.

"Yep," Tom said, giving an affirming nod, and returned to sorting tackle. After Lynn left the dock, Tom absent-mindedly took his felt hat from the bottom of the boat where he had set it, folded it, and put it in the small pack where he kept his rain gear. The resort grapevine carried the news about the luck of that man with a green hat.

The next morning Lynn didn't start fishing until 8 o'clock. The other boat was there, and the man told Lynn he had been on the water since 5 o'clock. The man departed from the spot in midmorning. Lynn came in at noon to check the fish shed. The waste barrel was again full.

"Why had that guy in the other boat gone out at 5 o'clock that morning to start fishing?" Lynn wondered. "Maybe he's following a moon chart" He shook his head in exasperation.

The two anglers shifted times and position on the reef again on Wednesday and Thursday. Lynn did not know what the other man had caught, but so far that week he had caught six rock bass and a sunny maybe weighing a pound.

On Friday both men were up before dawn and fished all day. The two of them circled and repositioned their boats throughout the hours of the day like two gladiators calculating each other's weaknesses. Lynn caught three more rock bass. He would play each fish for all it was worth, or, if caught on the rocks, give a full performance worthy of a ten pound walleye.

The man in the other boat was more circumspect. He would bring his fish in fast and, leaning over, take it off the hook in the water. Lynn felt a certain contempt for the secretive approach of his fishing neighbor. Lynn did not know, but the man caught and kept four rock bass on Friday—something to take home.

The next morning, Saturday, before they pulled out to go home both Lynn and the other man made reservations to come back the next year. Tom Yanich was in the lodge saying goodbye to his clients. After everyone had left, Tom sat in the lodge talking with Annie, the resort's owner.

Annie asked Tom, "You notice that farmer in the green seed cap and the guy with that olive-green canvas hat, lures stuck all over?"

"Yeah," said Tom, "fished the dead reef all the time."

"Yeah." Annie said. "They're both coming back next year. All they got all week were rock bass, and a sunny."

"You don't say," Tom marveled.

"Hey," Annie said, noticing the red hat next to Tom on the counter, "where's the old, green felt you usually wear. You didn't loose it did you. Everyone on the lake knows that hat."

"Umm," Tom looked down at the toe of his boot, "I gave it a rest this week."

PAULINE STEFFY

Light Stepping

I should like to dance
And at times I have imagined
What centuries come and past
Would do without light stepping

The wind will dance along the trees
The waves upon the shore
There is motion in all things I see
That are found in nature's store

What plays among the shadows
What sways us to and fro
What can make us waltz about
Or stumble
I should like to know.

Two Birds

I'll never know what moving force
Has made me feel this way
I only know that nature's course
Is by far the only way

One bird sat on my window
One bird sat on my tree
And I would wait each morning's break
For them to sing to me

"I'll sing to you a nesting song"
Said the bird up in the tree
And she murmured in her sweetest voice
"My love has come to me"

"My love has come to me" she sang
"My love has come to me"
And there never was a sweeter song
That was sung in any tree

Now the bird upon my window
Abruptly danced about
"I'll never understand" he said
"What these songs are all about"

"I'll keep the solo flight" he said
"I'll keep the solo flight
"For I enjoy the freedoms
"That are brought by morning's light"

Now I pondered what each bird had said
I pondered late and long
I thought about how much time had passed
Since I had sung a song

Well, "Where do I belong" I said
"By the window or the tree?
Will I enjoy a sweeter song
When my love has come to me?"

"When my love has come to me" I thought
"Should there be a song so true?"
But the lesson I have learned today
I will now pass on to you....

Talking birds are ridiculous
And this story isn't true.

MARGARET SWEET

The Velcro Cat

I was gone for a few days. That's an abnormal state of affairs around my house. I'm rarely gone overnight. My leaving is a traumatic event in the lives of my pets. They expect me at the same time every day—Kat sitting on the kitchen table where he knows he shouldn't be, and Ginger lying on a lawn chair on the deck waiting for his person's car to pull into the driveway. Both animals take great relish in my company on those days that I can stay at home all day.

At any rate, I was gone. Kat, the aging, slate-colored beast, would stay in the house. Ginger, the two-year-old who had moved in and stayed, would remain outside. This wasn't entirely pleasing to me, but I knew if I left him inside he would probably go out of his mind. Yes, he likes to come in each evening and spend the night on the foot of my bed. Yes, he loves to sit in the recliner with me and snuggle, purring his orange head off. No, he would not like to stay inside with Kat for several days and nights.

So off I went to enjoy a few days with loved ones leaving two very dependent animals behind, one on each side of the door. They weren't left unattended. My neighbor came daily to put fresh food and water out for them. She talked to Kat and petted him. She talked to Ginger, too, but he never came out to see her. He hid. She wasn't the right person.

I wondered, as I drove into my yard, what my reception might be. Sometimes pets will snub you when you come back after an absence. Sometimes they're just plain happy to see you. I soon found out. Kat, whom my neighbor had said stayed sprawled in the middle of the living room rug, was sitting on the kitchen table purring as I opened the door. No snubs here! But where was Ginger? I called, I looked, but no swaggering orange cat responded. All that evening I kept going to the door and calling, but no one answered. It was raining hard, and I was worried about my poor, stray kitty!

The next morning, even before I was up, I heard loud cries under my bedroom window. There he was! He rushed through the door talking steadily at me, and for the rest of that day and night, Ginger was a velcro cat. He was glued to my leg, my lap. Wherever I went or whatever I did, Ginger was there to do it, too. It took him a full twenty-four hours to realize that I was really home and to go back to his normal routine.

Don't ever let anyone tell you that animals don't have feelings, that they don't miss their people. I believe that they miss their people even more than they are missed.

Getting away was wonderful, but coming home to such a furry reception was sweetest of all.

ROBERT BEYMER

Destination Yet Unknown

She was born with Destination,
put on earth for special Purpose,
driven by a secret Motive,
lofty goals imbedded in her.

She is drawn to Mother Nature
energized by bolts of lightning,
tranquilized by wind and sunshine
on the hills of pine and aspen.

A Peninsula is like her,
joined to land by slender Isthmus,
sometimes flooded by the onset
of a tide that's overwhelming.

Stresses raise the tide around her,
and, alas, she is an island.
Isolation renders peace and
contemplation brings Direction.

Tide recedes from pure existence.
Island yields again to Isthmus.
Joined to land now she succumbs to
many pressures and temptations.

With distractions she does wander
off the path of most resistance.
She has strayed from destination—
—Destination yet unknown.

Idyll   Karin A. Hokkanen

If Only We Could be More Like the Chickadee

Autumn arrives early in the Northwoods. It is a season welcomed by mountain bikers and trail hikers, hunters and anglers. Walleyes and lake trout swim closer to the surface of crystalline lakes where wool-covered anglers find them with less effort. Biting insects retreat to secret haunts. Black bears prepare dens for long winter naps, no longer drawn to hanging food packs and garbage cans left out overnight. Moose stroll along the winding highways and narrow gravel roads, no longer hiding from summer's daily procession of RV's and canoe-topped automobiles. Tourists are at their homes. The streets of Ely are safe for roller-blading children who eagerly await the upcoming hockey season.

A favorite indication at our house that autumn has arrived is the return of our feathered friends to feeders that were not in use during the season of daily bear inspections. My favorite visitors are the chickadees. Other birds—pine and evening grosbeaks, other finches and sparrows—battle one another for position. Once established, they stay and eat and eat and eat until larger, more aggressive birds force them to leave. Not so with the cute little chickadees. A chickadee flies to the feeder, lands just long enough to select one sunflower seed, and then flies to a nearby branch where the tasty seed is delicately extracted from a protective shell. They are polite. They take turns. They mind their own business. And they don't bully others at the feeder.

If only human beings were more like chickadees...

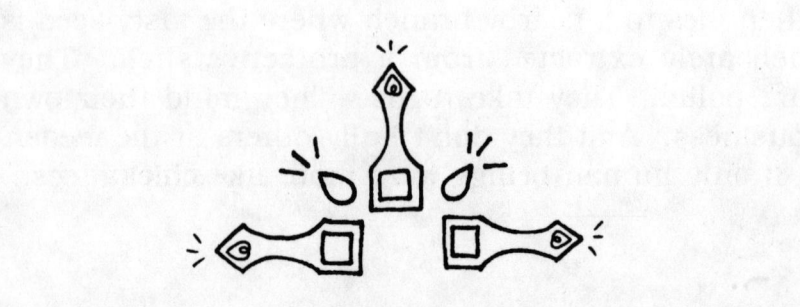

LOUIS BERNARD

The Exploding Barrel Stove

It was a sunny, late-fall afternoon, warm and quiet with a serious game of penny ante, three-card draw poker, going on in Barracks Number One. This Sunday the card table consisted of two footlockers set side by side, and upon it the six players were testing their luck.

The players, members of the Civilian Conservation Corps in 1937, had limited funds, so the bets were limited to ten cents. The pot now totaled thirty-eight cents.

Pete Ferris, a friend of mine, had won the last two hands, and a permissive glimpse at his present hand revealed only a pair of sixes. Pete knew I didn't play poker and wasn't worried about tipping his hand to me. Three players had already folded leaving only Tex Hochban, Blacky Burns, and Pete. Tex was debating whether to call or not. He looked at his cards again and folded.

Blacky called and Pete raised another ten cents. The son of a gun was bluffing! Could he win a third hand on nothing but a pair of sixes? Blacky paused, fingered his cards.

B-A-N-G!!!

Twelve feet of six-inch, tin stove pipe came clattering down in three-foot sections spewing soot and ashes which filled the air. The cast iron door of the stove, which was centered in the room, was torn from its hinges and hurled to the opposite wall of the room barely missing a man dozing in his bunk.

In this choking, acrid atmosphere, nine men madly scrambled for the nearest door resulting in a tangled mass of arms, legs, and bodies trying to exit all at once. And then, silence.

In the silence the soot and ashes slowly settled on

strewn cards and abandoned coins. Nine men had desperately fled for their lives, but two remained, Carl and I—the only two who knew what had happened.

Earlier that afternoon, Carl and I had decided to shave, but there was no hot water in the washroom after ten o'clock in the morning because the engine room man had the rest of the day off. So-o-o, if we wanted to shave, we would have to heat water in some way. No problem. We took an aluminum canteen, filled it with water, and put it into the barrel stove where a low, smoldering fire still burned. Apparently no one had noticed this because the card game was the center of attention.

The game had also attracted the interest of Carl and me; so much so that we lost all sense of time. The canteen had been in the stove for perhaps a half-hour before it built up enough steam pressure to explode. When it did, my first thought had been to get rid of the evidence. I looked in the stove and saw the remains of the canteen laying in a flat sheet. Somehow I picked it up and slipped it under my jacket.

After a few minutes of quiet, someone carefully peeked in the door and inquired "What happened?" Then another head appeared and repeated the same question, "What happened?"

Because there were three other doors to the building, no one questioned our presence. Perhaps they assumed we had just entered by another door.

"What happened?" "What happened?" It was generally conceded there had been an explosion in the stove, but what had caused it?

Several explanations were advanced.

<u>Number one:</u> Some of the firewood had come from an area where the blasting of stumps had been done before the road was built. Had dynamite been mixed with the wood some way? No, it would not cause an explosion because dynamite would not explode under those con-

ditions. It would only burn.

Number two: Maybe a blasting cap had been mixed in with the wood. No, it was a safety practice with the blasting crew when they set off a series of blasts to count all the explosions thus providing a record of all spent materials.

Number three: Maybe some water got inside of the wood, a hollow piece, and blew up. Not accepted. No one had ever seen a piece of firewood with a quantity of water inside it.

Number four: Some of that wood was black ash, and the smaller pieces hadn't been split. It's a hard wood, and maybe the heat had built up tensions that caused it to explode.

The mystery was never explained and neither Carl nor I told what we knew.

As a result of the explosion, the fellows no longer stood around the stove talking as was their habit after meals. There lingered the possibility that it might happen again.

Today, sixty years later, there must be a grandfather or two, even a great grandfather, who cannot resist telling about the barrel stove explosion back in '37. His descendents hear the story every time he sees a barrel stove. No doubt he has his own theory about what happened.

I can hear him speculating, "I once knew of a moonshiner who used to hide a full bottle in a hollow log for his customer to pick up. It was a powerful brew, almost two hundred proof. Maybe...just maybe...."

LOUIS BERNARD

There Were Three

Coffee party on an October afternoon.
Six young women at Anna's.
Greetings: "Nice dress." "A new hat?"
Clothing piled on the bed.
Embroidered pillow cases.

Smell of dynamite.
Pick and shovel.
Shovel, shovel, shovel.
Mucking ore, one car, two cars.
"You are working too hard Eino."
"I will soon have another mouth to feed."

"Anna is pregnant!"
Motherly advice from a mother of one.
Much teasing, morning sickness,
Marta's new baby, colic and remedies.
"Anna, where is Eino working now?"
"He is working at the Laura."

Sweat, smell of sweat, sweaty back.
Sweaty hair, sweaty face.
Shovel, shovel, shovel.
"What do women talk about, Walter?"
"They are funny. You listen sometime."
"I'll be a good father."
"Timber, bring more timber."
"Lagging."

Warm, moist air smelling of spice cake.
Moisture clinging to windows.
Anna's good china—white table cloth.
"Sugar? Cream? More coffee cake?"
New recipes for coffee cake.

"When will the baby come, Eino?"
"I don't know. They come when they are ready."
"More timber. Place the caps."
More lagging.
Three hours to go.

The high cost of sugar.
"The *Daily Worker* says...."
"Eino is making good money now."
"We must go—time to fix supper."
"Goodbye. Take care of yourself, Anna."

Two hours to go.
Last car, make ready for the next shift.
Down the drift, a thud, strange sound.
Rumble, timbers shuddering, red ore from above.
Shifting, caps bending, "Run! Run! Too late!"
Crushing blackness, smothering weight.
Bones snapping.
"Anna! Our baby! Our baby!"

Lungs filling with red ore.
Breathing ore.
Blackness forever.
No more pain.

Red sunset on a white house.
Red sunset on white curtains, all red.

Party dishes done, supper to make.
"Everyone liked my cookies; Greta had three."
A wife should look pretty when her husband comes home.
"Where is Eino?" Waiting, waiting.
"The night seems darker tonight.
"How long must we wait, I and our baby?
"Patience. Waiting seems forever."

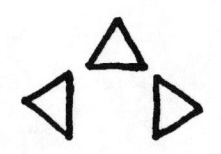

Night   Karin A. Hokkanen

BARBARA MURRAY

Legacy

In close circles
the mothertongues sang
from woman to woman to you

faint their singing has become
in their old hiding places
so soft, you can barely listen

then, stringing the long ago bow
gifted to you
a pluck vibrates into your center
and the grandmothers rise beside you
singing the tune of the deer giveaway
they practiced in prairie and woodland

you find it repeating in your blood
this timbre of the rhythm
as the pull of the arrow awakens tears of gratitude
for the remembrance of the circles of women
  chewing sinew
to soften and perfect your pull

grandmothers open your posture
lighting your belly to sprout the seed
of the strength you gained from knowledge
they drummed into your bones

the heart of this deer facing you
sends a welcome
as these women steady your aim
then crouch around your feet

this deer waits in offering, wanting to be part
of the blood of you and the mothers
and grandmothers

your aim is straight
filling your mouth
helping you live to not forget

every woman's blood lines of history.

BARBARA MURRAY

Woodcutter

chants clap through the forest
clattering, knocking bones sliced into the river

night hisses onto crystalline fields
carrying cold in its breath

the chimney sickens at its work
knowing the one out in the shadows
will raise her arms to lean oak against the flames
and the heat strikes back hard

those chants rise and drum
silences still and recede
as an iced blade shakes down raw
then turns over again in the two hands
of a night drummer leaning back in the forest
cracking logs open with an awareness that oak gives
its life over to heat.

DAWN DEWITT

Christmas Up North Where the Real Men Are

When my daughter and her husband invited me to spend the Christmas Holiday with them in Ely, Minnesota, I would never have guessed that my Bohemian son-in-law would choose that time to embark upon a never-to-be-forgotten project with an added never-to-be-forgotten surprise ending.

Louie is a second generation inhabitant of the great Boundary Waters area that separates the far northeastern tip of Minnesota from Canada. The Boundary Waters is a chain of interconnected lakes and rivers interspersed with dense forest and underbrush providing protective cover for all manner of wildlife where many like Louie can not imagine making a living or feeding his family by any means other than the age-old hunting and trapping.

During my late autumn visit to Ely, an elderly couple telephoned my daughter's home seeking Louie's help with a bothersome bear shot only minutes earlier on their property. They were unable to move their 400-plus pound bear out of the woods to a place of safety, and according to my daughter, Heather, had called the right outdoorsman for a much needed helping hand. Intrigued, my daughter and I gathered her son, Jordan, and arrived at the cabin by separate car just in time to see my son-in-law emerge from the woods dragging with sheer brute strength this massive black-coated bear. The bear was destined to either cover the floor of their cabin or perhaps cover the wall to keep out the Arctic winds.

The elderly couple invited us into their orderly, eat-off-the-floor-clean, year-around cabin home. They plied us with special cookies from old country recipes and explained their use of steaks, burgers, and sausage gleaned from the bear. Heavily accented chatter sprinkled with unmistakable thank yous and jubilant, broad smiles indicated excitement at this latest adventure. As we ate cookies and visited, they spoke of their rug-to-be. Clearly their relationship had been forged over time with Louie, and he relished sharing with them in this joyous occasion.

Three months had passed since my October visit, and Ely, the small timber and mining community in the Boundary Waters where my daughter and Louie lived, was deeply blanketed in the fresh, white, heavy snow. Tree branches were laden in picturesque fashion this Christmas week. At his home, Louie removed sixteen and one-half pounds of filleted fish from the freezer on Monday, five days before Christmas and announced matter-of-factly that he planned to can the fish.

For the following five days the ice-hardened fish melted, thawed, and became increasingly mushy as a tinged pool of dark liquid began encircling the base of the refrigerator interior and dripping into and onto all items within its path.

During the next several days, Louis regularly stuck his head into the refrigerator examining thoughtfully with his eyes and sometimes poking with a forefinger the yet hard but slowly thawing mass. Waiting expectantly for a comment, a sign, a signal indicating he might proceed with the canning project, I watched and wondered withholding to the point of almost bursting my question as to when the event might begin.

As house guest and mother-in-law, I prided my valiant success at maintaining silence. "The icy mass is too long thawed," I reasoned. Surely my son-in-law would come to this same conclusion. He didn't. The canning process would begin at a time and date know only to Louie.

The precise time was eight o'clock on the evening of

December 25th. Christmas dinner clean up was completed; the final traces of brightly colored gift wrap with trailing ribbons were discarded. The baby was tucked in for the night. It was a perfect, snowy evening to review the people, places, and tradition of holidays past, I thought. Soft radio music from WELY was regularly interrupted with newscasts of blizzard-like weather conditions. White outs promised several more inches of snow to be added to the already great mounds. Fierce winds causing the windchill factor to range from 40 to 55 degrees below zero were predicted. A grave-voiced radio announcer repeated often the admonition to venture outside only in an emergency.

At eight o'clock Louie began filling kettles with water. He washed and added the fish, vinegar, and spices. By midnight my nose ran constantly from the combined odors of vinegar and fish wafting from the kitchen and covering every square inch of their sizable up-north home. I had long since retreated to the guest room and tucked an extra blanket on the floor to keep the odors from entering at the base of the door. Finally I stuffed a wad of tissue into the keyhole, all to naught. The home, including my bedroom, took on all the combined odors and allowed me no escape.

The radio announcer offered more ominous weather warnings as midnight approached. Neither opening a window for a breath of fresh air nor going for a drive was an option. Restaurants, shops, and even the gas stations were closed. Helplessly trapped, I continued to cough and sputter, eyes watering, knowing if I did venture out I'd probably freeze—and really, who would find me? I suspected the police and even the snow plowing crews were at home sleeping, waiting for the sky to completely empty its bountiful offering of snow brought by the wind and arctic cold.

Better judgement nudged me toward patiently riding out the storm. Napping between incessant coughing and nose blowing episodes, I was suddenly wakened by the ear piercing wail of eighteen-month-old Jordan, who, if he could have talked, would probably have said "that odor is terrible." His top-of-the-lungs wail meant "I'm miserable! You fix it!"

The time was now 2:15 a.m. I questioned the merits of heading toward the nursery. Had I done so, I would have missed the best part of the entire holiday. For at that moment, on the stairs I heard muffled footsteps. Knowing the significance of the cry, Jordan's dad was coming to rescue his son and to fix whatever needed fixing. I remained quiet. The crying ceased, and I marveled at what a hero was this father of Jordan, my son-in-law at whom I was so furious earlier.

How did he fix it? He fixed all the household problems that night by simply turning off the burner. He quit the canning process in the middle of the night: no more boiling vinegar and fish. Then he proceeded to change, comfort, and gently rock his first born, baby boy singing softly into his tiny ear, the ear listening for vital man sounds, codes known only to the two of them. Baby quietly rested on his father's shoulder, one ear straining to hear the familiar heartbeat, the other listening for familiar sounds spoken from father to son.

Male bonding some call it. I call this the Olympic Event of Real Men, and with it comes the promise of their future.

JOHN DAVID

Three Wise Moose

Today is Christmas Eve, 1995, in Ely Minnesota. My friends and relatives in Baltimore, from where I migrated almost three years ago, think I'm insane enduring a pioneer existence in these far northern woods. They have concluded that I live out on Moose Lake Road in a mud hut, surrounded by bears and wolves, drawing my water through the lake ice, washing my clothes in a stream, and cooking wild game that I have killed with a bow and arrow.

The reality is somewhat different. Although it is snowing outside, the house is warm and toasty from my wood stove and my backup propane furnace. There is a frozen turkey, soon to be my Christmas dinner, nestled in the chest freezer. I won it last week playing bingo. I don't even own a bow and arrow.

As I write this piece on one computer, the other one is playing a compact disk of arias from Puccini operas. The dishwasher is busy washing the dishes. The dryer is drying the laundry. Life is good—as long as I pay my electric bill every month.

I wonder what sort of adventure I'm going to have tomorrow, Christmas day. Last Christmas day was beautiful. It was cold and sunny and everything in the woods was coated with a thick blanket of snow. I remember that at about 9 o'clock in the morning I got a yen for breakfast, specifically a Number Six breakfast from Britton's Cafe in town. I stuffed the dogs into the truck and headed into Ely. It never occurred to me that Britton's might be closed on Christmas morning and that I ought to call first. After all, Christmas is a day of faith.

Surprisingly, there was another truck on the Fernberg

Road, also heading into town. I decided to poke along behind him and enjoy the scenery. About a half mile after I passed the parking lot at Wood Lake, the road began a long descent to the Madden Creek area. At the bottom of the hill there was a rapid ascent, with stone walls on the right and Madden Creek somewhere out in the woods to the left.

As we were proceeding through this area, the truck in front of me suddenly slowed and then pulled into the center of the road and halted. I noticed that there was a van parked on the right side of the road just a few feet in front of the truck. A man and woman were standing in front of the van, staring at something farther down the road. I thought at first that there had been an accident. I pulled into the empty left lane and parked parallel to the truck. Now I could see what had everyone's attention, and it wasn't an accident; it was three bull moose.

All of them still had their antlers from the rut. Two of them were young moose and the antlers they sported were nice, but nothing sensational. Ah, but the third fellow was fully mature and the set that he had would have frozen any moose hunter in his tracks. He looked just like the label on a bottle of Moosehead Beer.

All three moose were facing east, obviously towards Bethlehem. Two of them were kneeling down in the middle of the road, their hind parts stuck up in the air in typical, ungainly moose fashion. The third was standing behind the others just at the road side. They were totally preoccupied, licking salt from the plowed road surface, oblivious to our presence just twenty-five yards away.

It is not easy for a moose to kneel down. After all, they have all that bulk perched atop those spindly legs. Watching the process is like watching the careful folding of a wooden deck chair upon which has been thrown a dark, shaggy blanket. In stages, and with great care, the moose gradually descends from upright down to ground level.

Given that it was Christmas, I began to think about the Three Wise Men who bore their gifts of frankincense, gold, and myrrh. For a good fifteen minutes we four humans stood in the silence of the forest watching that incredible scene, each of us lost in private thought.

There is something wonderful about confronting a wild animal in its own environment that can not be easily explained, especially to people who are city dwellers. Those who receive their dosages of animal exposure via the zoo or TV nature shows miss the emotional experience of the actual encounter.

Here were these three creatures in the presence of their most dangerous adversary blandly replacing lost sodium ions as we stood nearby. Ordinarily every molecule in their bodies would be screaming for them to run, to take flight and protect themselves from certain death at the hands of man. But they didn't. They tolerated our presence and continued licking the salt. We humans stood rooted to the spot, watching the trio ignore us as they went about the business of their survival.

In the snowy hush of the woods my mind was racing, picking up and discarding thoughts, images, and metaphors to describe the scene: Christmas day; Three Wise Men plodding to the east; Three moose facing east; animals in the stable clustered around the newborn.

At that moment the Philistines arrived upon our biblical tableau—two carloads of them. Seven or eight, in their early twenties, emerged from within their stopped cars.

"What are you doing?" the first one out yelled.

"Hush," I said. "Quiet! You'll scare the moose," I was ready to strangle him, never mind Christmas.

A girl came up. "Oh, aren't they cute?"

At this point we had a regular assemblage watching

the moose. Undeterred by our growing numbers, they continued their slurping and slobbering. It really was a day for miracles.

Suddenly a car loaded with the young Philistines passed me doing about twenty miles an hour. Appalled, I realized that they had reached the limit of their interest after about two minutes, and they were now rushing to go wherever it is that young Philistines are always rushing to go. The second car was running on the rear bumper of the first. Together they bore down on the unsuspecting moose. There was no way to stop them. They were going to zoom right up to our shaggy new friends.

Suddenly the moose became aware that all was not tranquil in paradise. Alarmed, they began unfolding those deck chairs as fast as they could go. The young Philistines never slowed, and the moose scattered just in time, two to the left and one to the right.

In an instant they were all gone, our show and their tormentors. Without saying a word the four of us got back into our three vehicles and drove away. What was stunning for one generation was delay for another.

So tomorrow is Christmas day again. Should I give it another try? After all, it is supposed to be a day of faith. The moose probably won't show, but on the other hand the Philistines probably won't show either.

Two fried eggs, over easy. Two pieces of toast. Hash brown potatoes with a lot of catsup. A piece of ham. A hot mug of coffee. I already feel the siren call of a Number Six breakfast.

Man, that Big Daddy moose had a great set of antlers.

BECCA BRIN MANLOVE

Picnic

Strolling
out onto
a grand
expanse
of frozen
lake,
a slice of
snow and
ice
spread
liberally
with sun
glaze
I find
myself
the ant
in
Today's
picnic.

Hauling Water

I fell in love with a man whose light blue eyes crinkle at the outer corners when he smiles. When I married Mike in the fall of 1988, I knew I was accepting a package deal: a husband, a job as caretaker of a camp on the edge of the Boundary Waters Canoe Area Wilderness, and Belfry.

Belfry, the caretaker's home, was a one-room cabin with a sparse 16 by 16 feet of floor space. A man named Bell had built it, hence the name "Belfry." Instead of perching on the steeple of a church, the cabin rested on cement blocks on one side; on the other side where the blocks had sunken into the ground a round log was used as a spacer which gave the cabin a ready-to-roll look that was not very reassuring. Belfry had charming, many-paned windows with matching storm windows, a gas heater, and electricity. The "water system"—a large, galvanized steel garbage can with a spigot welded near the bottom—took up one-third of the tiny kitchen counter.

The can held about 20 gallons of water, which we tried to make last as long as possible. When our supply gave out we loaded the can onto a long, wooden toboggan. Four of the other winterized cabins had the same system. If Mike and I had guests coming, we loaded the sled with two or three cans at a time. One of us pulled the toboggan along the curving paths to the lake while the other followed to reload any containers that fell off.

The noise we made depended on the weather. Fresh, soft powder muffled the tramping of our heavy Sorel boots and absorbed the rattling of the metal containers.

Cold of -30 degrees Fahrenheit or more caused the snow to squeal under our rubber soles, and the metallic clanking of the cans rang through the air. Toward spring, the hard-packed trails began to melt. Our boots muttered low and wet while the sled made a whooshing sound over the track.

Each winter, about 15 yards from shore we thrust a piece of lathe into the snow with a cardboard sign—"water." On top of the tilted post we upended a battered but shiny aluminum cooking pot without handles. When the ice was about six inches thick, we chopped a hole in it about a foot in diameter, covered the hole with a piece of plywood, and then piled snow on top of the board for insulation. We thrust a snow shovel and a slender, red ice chisel into the snow next to the sign. Whenever we hauled empty water cans onto the lake, everything we needed was there. Mike grabbed the shovel and removed the pile of snow from the plywood. I pried up the board with the tip of the ice chisel. Occasionally, in warm weather the hole would be open, but most often the water lay black under a film of ice. Once the film was shattered, the water took on the quality of the light. On bright, clear days we could see to the bottom of the lake—the warm, golden color of the sand stark contrast to the cold white all around us. The thickness of the ice could be seen, which in cold winters might be fourteen inches or better. The bottom edge sparkled sharp and clear like broken glass.

One winter, the ice chisel slipped from an icy leather chopper into the hole. We could see it laying on the gently rippled sand—bright and taunting—whenever we broke the ice and thrust the chisel's replacement, a heavy, dull spudbar, back into the snow.

Once the ice was broken, I hesitated before I knelt down beside the hole because I knew I would soon have a wet knee and damp hands.

Our dipper was the shiny aluminum pot. Often, it was

coated with a thin sheet of ice. I rapped the pot sharply against the shovel handle to crack and crumble the coating. Grasping the dipper in one mittened hand (we wore "choppers"—leather outers with tightly woven woolen liners) and leaning on my other hand, I reached down into the hole and pushed the pot down into the water. Ice chunks swirled and slid as the water streamed into this new empty space. The pot held only two quarts. I filled it as full as possible, then lifted it quickly, trying not to let too much water spill out, before I tipped it over the lip of the nearest garbage can. Again and again, I bent, filled, lifted, and poured. When at last the container was nearly full, I poured more slowly to avoid getting splashed, and the water streamed in a sheet that reflected the sunlight.

Mike put the container's lid on firmly and slid the toboggan forward so that the next can was nearest the hole while I stood up. Sometimes, the knee of my wool pants would be frozen to the ground. I would pull it up gently, leaving behind black or green lint in an oval pattern on the ice, and the frozen cloth bumped against my shin each time I took a step. Mike took his turn at kneeling and filling. On very cold days the first container had a thin sheet of ice on top by the time we filled the last one.

When, at last, all the containers were filled we played our game—we were newlyweds after all. One of us stepped into the rope of the sled and held it at waist height. The other stood at the side of the sled and, holding onto the two rear lid handles, yelled "Mush, you husky! Hike!" The "husky" howled and yapped, then lunged forward. A hard snap on the rope was needed to get the sled moving when it was loaded, and we had to gain momentum to get up a slight rise from the lake. The "musher" kept a firm press on the lids of the rear cans and ran alongside. If the sled slid over to the side of the trail, the "musher," was forced off into the deep snow and had to flounder through, trying to keep up and hold the cans on at the same time. We yelled "Hike," and howled between gasps of laughter until the toboggan burst from the trail onto a wide, firm road. The water sloshed heavily and rocked the cans with sudden leveling off.

To deliver each container, we pulled the sled along narrow trails that led in to the cabins. We stopped the sled as close as we could to the steps. Standing on either side, we each grasped a handle and lifted. Since I am six inches shorter than Mike, I went up the stairs backwards, straining to lift my side of the heavy can with each step up. Mike kept his side level with mine and followed me up the stairs and through the doors. We shuffled quickly across the kitchen, our steps shortened by the weight of the water and the awkward bulk of the can between us. At the count of three, we lifted it up and onto the counter with the spigot jutting out over the sink.

I weighed just over 100 pounds then, and carrying and lifting the water was a strain that I dreaded. Usually, I lost my sense of humor by the third can. Adrenalin from anger sometimes helped me finish the task.

Often, after we had lifted a frosty garbage can into place, Mike lifted the lid off the can and looked in. I stood on tiptoe and peered in, too. Water that had been in the container for a few days had a fishy smell, but freshly-hauled water had a clean, cold scent like snow.

There was no reason to look inside the can. The level of water didn't matter because we wouldn't haul more water to add to it at that point. And leaks were more obvious from the outside. We lifted the lid because the cold scent and the full dark measure of the water, with chips of ice tinkling on top, was a reward for our efforts.

The time and effort that water hauling took made water precious. When I felt the weight of each gallon, it was easy to believe that the amount of potable water in the world had a measure, too. And each drop was something to celebrate.

KARIN HOKKANEN

A Winter Memory

When the winter chill turns so cold that my words freeze before they reach my friend's ears, I recall the winter that I spent at a folk high school in southern Finland. I was teaching English part-time and receiving room, board, and tuition in return. Teachers viewed me as a student, and the young students viewed me as an instructor, a situation that led to a dilemma one particular winter evening.

A mid-winter dance had been announced for Saturday in the town about eight miles away. I wanted to go. Two difficulties stood in my dancing path: transportation and school policy. The public buses didn't run at the necessary times, so I opted to use the heavy-duty Russian made bicycle that I had purchased several months earlier. The first situation solved, I turned my thoughts to the second, a bit stickier since students were allowed to go dancing only when they were on leave time. I lived at the school and had no place to go home to. Rather than making a scene about the student/teacher status with the administration, I rather headstrongly declared myself on a weekend vacation and secretly hoped someone would leave a late night door open.

When the dance evening approached, I began to regret my stubbornness in going for the temperature had dropped to -15 degrees Fahrenheit by the time I wanted to leave. With growing apprehension, I tied my bundle of high heels, dress, and make-up kit on the bike rack while I already shivered a bit in my snowsuit and boots. With the bike helmet strapped over a bulging knit hat, I felt—as well as looked—like an alien.

The road to town wound through farm fields and deep woods, through little villages and up hills and down. Normally the ride would have taken about half an hour, but the cold temperature was causing the Russian oil in the bicycle gears to gum up making pedaling almost impossible and doubling the trip time.

When I finally reached the dance hall, I was out of breath, a little grumpy, and red-faced from the bite of the cold. Well, no matter, time to warm up and change into my dancing clothes and spin a bit on the beautiful hardwood floor.

The live music seemed to speed up the clock as the *pelimanni* band reeled out the waltzes, tangos, humppas, and an occasional polka and schottische. I was having a great time when before I knew it, the last waltz was being played, and the crowd was thinning into the night. As the band packed their instruments and the custodian began sweeping the floor, I made my way to the restroom where I exchanged my dress up fancies for the bulky insulation I needed for the return ride.

With a melody still humming through my blood, I, too, turned out into the night, found my bicycle, and began slowly waltz pedaling on my way. The bright lights of town abruptly ended in darkness with the last suburban house, and the forest began to close in soon after. A light snow had fallen, and I could barely see the road. The bicycle generator wouldn't work with the build up of snow on the tires. In one low area I pedaled into a deep fog, keeping to what I thought was the middle of the road and hoping in my rising panic that no early morning driver would come speeding my way. Once out of the heavy mist, I could see an occasional light in the distance from a farmhouse or other backwoods dwelling.

I continued in the center of the asphalt, the darkened strip leading me onwards through the winter whiteness. The temperature had dropped, and now in the dark calmness, the only wind I could hear was my own labored breathing in going up the last big hill. My toes were numb and fingers were chilled, and I truly wondered whether the dancing had been worth this travel folly, but as I nudged out of the forest to the downward slope, the answer burst into a magnificent display of a million stars gleaming in the far northern sky. I held my breath suddenly and in that suspended moment felt the awesome touch of the universe. No noise sounded to break the crystalline beauty of that heavenly dome, just a young American on a Russian bicycle coasting into the star-studded elegance of a Finnish winter night.

MARGARET SWEET

I Remember

I remember that day my father died. It took me thirty-five years to be able to talk about it, but I do remember. My father and I had gone to Gheen to visit his friends at the railroad siding, and I was quietly playing by myself on one end of the room while he and the other men sat on benches at the long table drinking coffee and talking. I remember. I remember just like yesterday how, in slow motion, his coffee cup fell to the floor as he toppled sideways off the bench. I remember sitting very quietly until the wife of the siding manager came to take me to her home to wait for my mother. No one told me my father was dead. No one had to. I knew instinctively. I think children do somehow.

I remember the dimness of that living room where I sat on the rug and played with blocks until my mother came. I didn't cry. I don't recall ever crying about his death. Years later, my mother told me that hard as she tried to get me to talk about that awful day, I never would.

I do remember the day when I could finally talk to her about it. She cried tears of joy that my mind had finally released me from that tortuous memory. She shared her memory with me of the nightmares that haunted me for months after his death and her pain in not being able to reach me. I recall all through grade school and high school making up occupations for a mythical father whenever anyone asked me what he did. Call it denial, or whatever you want; I could not face his death.

It's strange how life changed in so short a time. When my father died, I was four years old. He worked for the Department of Natural Resources, and as this was February, he was laid off. I lived during the week with my father in our home in rural Orr.

My mother taught school in Greaney. She and my older sister lived all week in the teacherage of the two room school, coming home on weekends.

Greaney, a small farming community, was only a few miles away, but in those days it might have been a hundred miles. The road, at that time, did not run in a straight line. It twisted and turned, corkscrewing around corners and hitching its way up and down steep hills. It was a country road and, of course, unpaved.

Friday afternoon was my favorite time of the week. My father and I would drive to Greaney to pick up my mother and sister, making an anticipated stop along the way at the Gheen Coop Store to purchase a small brown paper bag of candy corn which we shared on the bone-jarring car ride to the Greaney school.

Sometimes on that trip, we stopped at my aunt and uncle's farm where I drank milk and ate my Aunt Irene's delicious cookies while the adults talked, coffee cups in hand.

Those weekends were so short and the frequent partings so painful that to this day I cannot recall them.

My mother was at work when the call came through that my father was dead. The school had no telephone, so the message was delivered by a woman who lived near the school, a home with a phone. Transportation had to be arranged and a substitute teacher located before my mother and my sister could be brought to Gheen where my father's body still lay on the wooden floor of the siding house.

After his death, my grandmother came to live with us and to keep house while my mother worked to support us all. She and my sister lived at home now, riding each day those rough roads in what passed for a school bus. This bus was a sort of van with benches along the sides and, in the winter, heated by a kerosene lantern. My mother didn't drive, and even if she had, there was still a war going on and gasoline was in short supply.

The memories ended the day my father died and were not revived until I was an adult with grown children of my own.

LYNN ROGERS

The Orphaned Cubs: A True Story

The cub wrapped his arms around my neck and held on as we snowmobiled along a scenic trail near Ely, Minnesota. He looked ahead into the warming April wind, and seemed to enjoy the only snowmobile ride he would ever have. He and his sister had been orphaned a month earlier in the Lower Peninsula of Michigan when hikers discovered their den, actually a surface nest. He and his sister had been born in this nest in January and had spent their first two months there snuggled under their mother. It hadn't taken the hikers long to realize this real mother was not the ferocious mother bear of books and folklore, and they returned day after day to photograph her. They made noises to get her attention. They prodded her with sticks so they could see the cubs nursing under her. She feared humans, and her fear grew as the people grew bolder. Finally, she left.

A Michigan game warden tracked her more than a mile, but the tracks led straight away—with no sign that she would return. By that time, the shivering cubs were within a few hours of dying, so he took them home and kept them warm and fed them from a bottle. The next day, wildlife officials began a search for wild mothers to adopt the cubs and raise them wild and free.

Mothers that have cubs of their own will adopt strange cubs until they leave the den, then they gradually become more discriminating and sometimes even kill strange cubs. The officials were trying to find wild mothers before it was too late—but after a month with no luck, the officials were getting worried. The cubs were getting so attached to people that they might not accept a wild mother. And it was already April. Bears were leaving their dens. The search for wild mothers expanded to other states.

Wisconsin bear biologist Bruce Kohn knew of a mother, but she was already out of her den. Still, it was the best chance they had, so they flew one of the orphans to him—the male. The mother saw the cub, investigated him, and knew he wasn't hers. She turned and walked away. Kohn picked up the cub, and the search extended to northern Minnesota where bears leave their dens a week later.

My phone rang. I said, "Yes, I have a couple of mothers that might be in their dens. Probably our best bet would be a mother I checked a couple weeks ago. She's 17 years old, weighs 175 pounds, and has two cubs. She's big enough to make milk for an extra cub. If the Minnesota Department of Natural Resources says it's okay, I'll take one of the orphans to her den and see if she'll accept it."

The next day, April 12, the officials flew to Wisconsin and picked up the rejected male and then on to the Ely Airport where I was waiting. They handed him to me. He was at the age when cubs can't get any cuter: blue eyes, nine pounds, and teddy bear fur. No one at the airport could resist petting him. He liked people and liked being held. I wondered if he could go back to being a bear. Within an hour he and I were snowmobiling to the old bear's den which was a surface nest like the one he had been born in.

When I stopped the snowmobile and the sound faded away, he loosened his hold on my neck and climbed higher, standing with his front paws on my head to look around. I balanced him as I turned on the radio receiver and pointed the directional antenna to see if the radio-collared mother was still there. She was. I set the orphan down on the snow, and started toward her through the woods. He tried his best to keep up as I carried the receiver and antenna into the woods. A couple hundred yards farther the mother's radio beeps grew stronger, and I saw her sitting in her nest behind the upturned roots and trunk of a fallen tree. She was looking back over her shoulder at me and the cub. At ten yards, she glanced nervously away. I stopped and gently picked up the orphan and tossed him halfway to the den.

He plopped in the snow and yelped. The mother leaped up, scrambled over the trunk, and rushed to him. She was making the grunting sounds mothers make when they're concerned about their cubs, but the cub didn't understand. In terror, he lay on his back and fought with all four little feet, yelling at the top of his lungs. She turned away, and the cub scampered back to me. The mother didn't dare follow. She looked at me and walked out of sight. Her two cubs lay quietly in her nest. I carried the orphan over and set him gently in with them. He stood and backed away from them, making the throaty sound bears make when they feel threatened.

I hurried away, hoping the mother would quickly return. Through the trees, I saw the cub leave the nest and climb a tree. I stopped and watched as the mother returned, checked her cubs, and climbed after him, again grunting her concern. He was too afraid to care what she was saying. He blew and chomped his jaws, trying his best to warn her away.

She climbed down and went to her den and disappeared through the trees with her two cubs behind her. It was clear she would have accepted the orphan, but the orphan was so unwilling, I was afraid she was giving up.

The next day I returned with my wife Donna. The orphan was high in a tree, and the mother and two cubs were resting 75 feet away, apparently waiting for him to join them. The mother stood up warily as we approached, and her two cubs started up a tree. When the orphan saw real people beneath his tree, he came down and climbed my leg. He was scared and probably lonely. It was more than a day since he'd eaten. I walked slowly toward the mother, peeled the cub off my pantleg, and tossed him toward her. He squalled and ran back to me. Then I picked him up and tossed him past the mother. He looked around and screamed. He couldn't get back to me without going past the mother. We hurried away to let him and the mother work out the problem alone.

The next day, the mother stood guard under a tree with three cubs in it. The orphan had finally accepted the mother's offer of warmth, food, and protection. He became a full-fledged member of the wild family. As much as he liked people, no one ever heard of him having anything to do with people again even though natural food was scarce that summer and fall. Berries were so hard to find that his two new brothers were among the many cubs that died that year. In October, he and his mother entered a den and snuggled together for the winter. The next spring, he stayed with her until it was time for her to mate again and she made it clear she wanted to be alone. By then she had taught him all he needed to know to find food, and she continued to give him protection by letting him stay in her familiar territory where other bears dared not stay for long.

I last saw him when he was two-and-a-half-years old, and he was probably about ready to leave his mother's territory and find a home of his own. By that time, I'd given him a set of numbered eartags so he could be identified if he ever were killed in his travels. He was now officially number NC-465. Over ninety percent of black bears are killed by people, so I knew there was a reasonable chance that someday I'd learn the end to his story.

On June 14, 1996, in the last hour of Ontario's spring bear season, NC-465 was killed at the age of seven and a half. Hunter Gerald Harman and his guide James

Malcolm read me the eartag numbers over the telephone and told me the kill location. The bear had moved 73 miles north northeast from his foster mother's territory, which is not an unusual distance for a male to travel before establishing his adult range.

The hunter and guide went on to describe a bear that had nearly lost his life twice before. Somewhere along the way, NC-465 had lost his left front leg at the shoulder--an injury that is often the result of a bullet. The skin was well healed over the shattered bone, and he still had an inch of fat left over from hibernation. The bear was making the best of his situation; but sometime in the last three weeks, he had had another narrow escape. Triangular shaped entry and exit wounds in his chest showed where an archer had aimed too far forward. Mr. Harman killed him cleanly.

Ironically, Mr. Harman was from the Lower Peninsula of Michigan. The thousand mile odyssy of NC-465 would end very near the bear's birthplace.

If you're wondering what happened to his orphaned sister, Gerry, she was adopted by another Ely bear and is still alive, but that's another story.

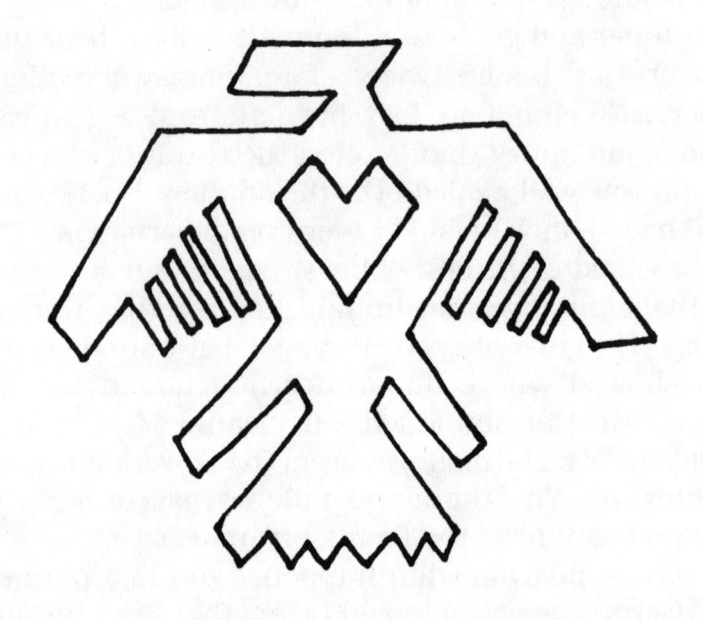

ANNE STEWART

Envisioning a Landscape: The View from Brunhilde's Rock

The outcropping of granite rock rises some thirty feet above the marsh and has a diameter across the top of seventy-five to a hundred feet. On cold winter days you can hunker down near the top on the protected south side of the rock, and even though the winter sun draws a low arc across the south horizon, the sun warms you on Brunhilde's rock .

The landscape visible to the south of Brunhilde's rock is grassy marsh extending more or less east and west, and beyond that, across the marsh, is a ridge with exposed rock cliffs crowned with red and white pines. A small stream meanders the length of the marsh. In the winter the indentations of our snowshoe trail are visible along the frozen course of the stream.

Sometime in late April the ice will melt and the stream will flow free. May brings flocks of warblers, and in a matter of days plants impulsively spring to life.

I turn and face the north side of Brunhilde's rock, a shear drop thirty feet down to the forest floor where anemone and star flowers blossom beneath pine and spruce trees. The land runs northward a hundred feet to a steep incline up to a ridge line of forest. The ground laid bare by melting snow is overrun with plant life, and the forest is brim full of bird songs. A purple finch, proudly decked for mating, sits in the tip top of a spruce at eye level with my rock perch and serenades me beautifully. I inhale and exhale deeply and breathe the life of my landscape, my home. For nearly three decades I walked the woodlands of northeastern Minnesota and paddled across its waters, and more and more I wanted to claim this landscape as my own. So I bought a piece of land, and now, here I sit on Brunhilde's rock. I have paid my money, and it is mine.

On a mid-summer's day I sit imbibing the scene; there seem to be others on my rock, and they are laughing at me. The forest has grown much older. The one hundred-year-old white pines scattered among the red pines on my land are yearlings in comparison to the mammoth whites spreading their branches across the sky of my mind's eye. I am an alien in some past time, or perhaps the future. I am not sure.

The ethereal presences sharing my rock take shape in my mind. They are clothed in skins and have the look of Native Americans. I am not sure if they are Dakota or Ojibwe. Their laughter increases as they mouth the clumsy word "Brunhilde." This word from a Wagner opera has no roots here. It floats from their mouths and bobbles ridiculously in the air. They don't accept how this rock landscape fits the Wagnerian stage. They don't picture the Germanized Norse Valkyrie, Brunhilde, decending on horseback from the sky and landing here with the fugitive Sieglinde, or the Norse god, Wotan, having it out with Brunhilde, his daughter, and leaving her asleep and captive, surrounded by a ring of fire. They contemptuously spit out the alien word I have given their rock, their landscape, and turn and pay homage to the bear walking below. Come winter, they will kill and eat it, first asking permission and paying honor to its spirit. I have no use for the bear, nor it for me. I am not bound to this land by need for food and shelter. I do not see it as a place for harvest.

On a fine fall day, when the colors are flaming up on the trees, my reverie atop Brunhilde's rock is broken by the sounds of chain saws and heavy machinery. I know that someplace across the marsh to the southeast beyond the ridge, the red and white pines are giving way to the bite of the saw. Man-made machines are gripping whole trees and uprooting them in one swift move. With paranoid intensity I wait for the machines to stride over the ridge like Wagner's giants, Fasolt & Fafner, and demand payment in gold. The machines do not appear because the owner of the land that abuts mine to the south is a trapper. He lives snug in the middle of his forty, living off the hides of the beaver, marten, mink, ermine, and fox that inhabit his and the adjoining State land. He holds on to his trees, does not sell out to the logger. But he does not begrudge the logger. Both lay claim to working to survive off the land. I, too, work to survive off the land—by writing, taking in its drama and beauty as my sustenance. Now, I draw lines between my trapper neighbor, the logger, and me.

At the town hall people are drawing lines and making rules about how land will be used. The Town Planning and Zoning Committee is holding an open meeting. I am surprised to see my neighbors who live lakeside. They have come to the meeting to request stricter regulations and larger lot size requirements for the land across the lake from theirs—the land that they view from their windows. They fear their view of now uninhabited shoreland will become cluttered with closely spaced cabins and unfettered human activities. Heated discussion follows. An official claims built-in protection against crowding is guaranteed by septic and setback requirements. My neighbors argue that developers can circumvent the requirements. A real estate agent bemoans the diminishing amount of available land for development and contends that keeping lot sizes big shuts out some people from owning lakeshore land.

Land use debates have haunted the Arrowhead Country for more than seventy years. In September, 1925, the issues were defined in a courthouse hearing room in International Falls when two strong-willed men squared off. Edward Backus and Ernest Oberholtzer presented their opposing visions of the landscape along the Minnesota/Canadian border to the International Joint Commission—a commission created by the U. S. and Canadian governments to settle border disputes.

Backus and Oberholtzer lived on neighboring islands in Rainy Lake. Backus was an energetic entrepreneur who had built the pulp and paper industry at International Falls and Fort Frances. An industrial harvesting of resources and economic development were the images that played on the stage of Backus' vision. Backus had built dams on Rainy Lake at Koochiching Falls and at the inlet from Namakan Lake. He envisioned dams all along the border from International Falls to Saganaga Lake. He saw the area as an immense hydropower resource for the pulp, paper and hydroelectric power industries. His plan involved raising water levels as much as thirty feet and turning the border lakes into reservoirs. It meant the drowning of islands and waterfalls including Lower Basswood Falls.

Oberholtzer, a Harvard graduate and landscape architect, had a different vision. He loved the natural beauty of the north country. He had first come in 1909, at age 19, after he was told he had a short time to live. He regained his health canoeing the boundary waters. Like Thoreau, Muir, and other lovers of wild places, he had found a spiritual habitat in the wilderness.

Now, in 1925, Oberholtzer was concerned about the effect of dams and development. He conceived a plan to preserve the border country as a wilderness place and presented his plan to the commission. Others shared his vision and joined him in the struggle to create a wilderness area on both sides of the United States/Canadian border.

The struggle shifted to Congress, and in 1930 a first victory was won. The Shipstead-Nolan Act was passed. The Act prohibited logging within four hundred feet of shoreline and curtailed the raising of water levels above the natural levels on certain lakes.

Backus died in 1934, but Oberholtzer worked for another thirty years to secure his vision, and in 1964 the Wilderness Act was passed by Congress. The Act determined the landscape of wilderness we have today in the Arrowhead country of Minnesota, but it did not settle the dispute.

In the town hall the dispute continues. A slim, white-haired woman, a longtime resident and former town board member, spews energy and irritation as she shakes a finger at my neighbors.

"You say 'developer' as if its a bad word," she chides. She talks about a tax base and the need for jobs for those who live here—many of them fourth generation descendants of immigrants who came here as miners and lumberjacks before anyone designated it wilderness. The former board member warms to her topic. The government as intruder and land owner that adds nothing to the local economy is part of her litany of hindrances to true development. My lakeshore neighbors are chagrined and even apologetic. They do not know about federal contributions or non-contributions. They cannot argue back.

They might have argued that the federal government does contribute to the local economy through payroll for Forest Service personnel; that it covers the cost of management of federal lands for wildlife, recreation, and use of resources; that it allows private loggers to take timber—a positive contribution to the local economy. Lakes protected from polluters and protected forest lands attract retirees, summer residents, and tourists who contribute large sums of money to the local economy.

The federal government makes payments in lieu of taxes (PILT) to the state for all federally held land. Payments range from seventy-five cents to three dollars per acre.

The white-haired woman will have something to say: "Land used for homesteads, businesses, and industry generate far more tax revenue for local units of government than do PILT payments. Commercial and residential property may bring in $500, $1000 or more per acre."

To develop or not to develop. "Ah, there's the rub." Over this dilemma of Shakespearean proportion we "strut and fret" and do battle with each other. The front line of the battle: The U. S. Forest Service versus Cook County, and vice versa. The County wanted to trade much of the 2,500 acres of land it has in the Boundary Waters Canoe Area Wilderness (BWCAW) for land the Forest Service had outside the BWCAW. As part of the trade, the County wanted 35 acres of land the Federal Government leases to three resorts in the Gunflint Trail corridor and to one resort on the Sawbill Trail. The Gunflint corridor is land along either side of the Gunflint Trail—a road that extends about fifty miles into the BWCAW. If Cook County received the acreage in the corridor, the county planned to sell the land to the resort owners. From the County's point of view, this would boost county tax revenue on those acres.

The County requested that in the trade it receive land equal in value to what it would give up. The Forest Service agreed to an equal value trade if the acreage in the Gunflint Corridor was not involved. The Forest Service wants to keep control of the 35 acres because within it are access points to the BWCAW. The Forest Service wants to be certain that use of the land does not compromise the surrounding wilderness.

"We are supportive of current use by those leasing the land, and we have no plans for canceling any leases," a spokesperson said, "but resorts change hands. What if sometime in the future someone puts in bungee jumping?"

The County counters that because resort owners do not own the land, they cannot use the land as collateral to obtain bank loans for expansion and the future of the resort is always dependent on decisions of the Forest Service.

What this confrontation is really about is where the

lines will be drawn between wilderness and nonwilderness uses. Those individuals and groups who want private development and multiple use of forest land see the Forest Service's refusal to give up the 35 acres as a move to grab even more land, close the corridors into the BWCAW, and expand the wilderness to who knows where—maybe clear south to Pine County.

Groups and individuals who want to limit use and preserve the wilderness return the suspicions of their opponents in equal measure. Friends of the Boundary Waters, an organization dedicated to the preservation of the BWCAW as wilderness, is certain that Conservationists with Common Sense (CWCS) wants to open the whole of the BWCAW to logging and motorized boat and airplane use. Friends and CWCS went to court over motorized transport of boats over Prairie Portage in the BWCAW—a battle that was the epitome of turning mountains into molehills. The Friends testimony included reference to an old basketball hoop stuck on a tree and used by the the twin daughters of the family who ran the portage truck-crossing operation. CWCS gleefully played up the Friends gaffe as anti-youth and with exaggerated righteousness took up the cause of the aged and disabled who they claim cannot travel the BWCAW without motorized transportation. Where the infirm can go by motor, all others can follow.

As I watch the finger shaking and listen to the debate taking place in our small town hall, I wonder what landscape vision each of us sitting there has, and what life vision. Does the white-haired woman want to see Edward Backus' landscape become a reality? Does she want cemented landscape, smog, dirty rivers and lakes, violent crime, and incessant traffic noise that will smother the sounds of songbirds, the loon, the wolf? She will say I am being absurd, that it is not possible for such development to take place here.

She will ask me what modern conveniences I am

willing to forego. Do I want television, my roads repaired, electricity, fire protection, law enforcement? Do I want a home made of wood, paper to write on? Once the argument is started it can go on and on as it does in town halls, city halls, public meeting places, and courtrooms across the Northland.

Perhaps this is the proper way—for all of us to continue to bicker, confront, contend, and compromise. Maybe this is the way for each of us to have a little piece of what we need. Perhaps we need to keep drawing lines, keep debating. But each of us inhabits this world for a short period of time. The earth will go on without us for some eons to come. How will we leave it for the next occupants, and the next, and the next?

I lie back on Brunhilde's rock and watch an airplane overhead. The people in the plane can see me and my landscape and the far flung landscape inhabited by trappers and loggers, resort vacationers, canoeists, and even merchants in town. Somehow it all fits together for today and for ourselves.

For tomorrow and for those who may come to Brunhilde's Rock then, what do we leave? I hear them coming from the future, clambering up the rock face toward those of us who dwell in the past. I want to leave them an offering. I want to leave them the eternal sound of waterfalls, the lakes where humans have canoed and bathed for centuries, the forest where for generations we have greeted the bear and spoken with the wolf. I want to leave them this rock where a purple finch decked out for mating still sings his song. I want to leave them the silence to hear and see these things.

If we are to leave all of this for a future world, we must be very careful where we draw lines on the landscape.

ROBERT BEYMER

The Best and Worst of Times

Spring: Charles Dickens would surely describe it as the best of times, the worst of times.

Either way, Spring is a quiet time in Ely, Minnesota. A tourist town feels empty when tourists stay home. There is not much reason to visit the Northwoods in springtime. The remaining snow, clinging to the north slopes of pine-covered hills, is poor for cross country skiing and snowmobiling. Lakes are frozen, but ice has blackened, too weak to walk on, too thick for boating. Fishing and hunting are not in season. Back roads and trails are muddy. Branches of birch and aspen trees are bare, as they have been since mid-October.

No, Spring is not appreciated by those who play outdoors. Perhaps the best thing about it, to many, is anticipation of the fishing opener just around the corner. We take comfort in knowing that it is the Northwoods' shortest season—the month of April, give or take a few days.

Spring is, nevertheless, a time for renewal, arousing hope and anticipation in even the gloomiest of souls. Nowhere is this renewal more evident than in the deep woods of the North country. Rivers shackled by ice since November once again run free, now faster and fresher than ever. Bald eagles pluck fish from the cold, clear water below bubbling rapids. Yawning black bears squint at sunlight not seen since autumn. Peppy purple finches and slate juncos replace common redpolls and boreal chickadees at the feeders. Occasional robins are seen on yards and open fields, where patches of green grass emerge on sun-drenched glacial soil.

Spring is also a time for reflection. One mild, sunny

late-April afternoon, I rested on a small rock outcrop along the Kawishiwi River. Watching a young deer tiptoe through a black spruce grove near my home, I was struck by how fortunate we are to live in a place considered by many to be among the most beautiful in the nation. A tourist with camera pointed toward the scenic river setting stands on a bridge that I cross each and every day. While eating lunch in a city park, I gaze upward to watch three bald eagles soaring high above our town. Awakened by bright sunlight on a calm, summer morning, an impulse leads to lunch on the rocky shore of a pristine lake within the Boundary Waters wilderness. It's a destination planned for months by other canoeists seen nearby.

Yes, fortunate we are. If only we can make it through Spring.

BARBARA MURRAY

Morning

the silent grey
of morning cracks
with the light it is
a time of subtle patterns

thoughts striving toward formation
dreams running away
the dawn lumbering off toward China

it is a time of dread
of leaving the mist and quietness
surrounding your body

BARBARA MURRAY

Desert Dreamtime

thundering mesa, black luminosity
the mother
speaking up all day
chasing silence away
she readies

golden and vibrant
sky opens his arms
reaching down to her

with the day pulling back
he presses red lips against her side
crouching, rides lined shadows
around her, merging her dreamtime with his.

A Saint Patrick's Day Poem in the Evening

Blowing around my emerald dress flutters
Gentle breezes' kiss on St Patrick's day.
Sitting at the Boulderado Hotel, Colorado traveling
Through eons of sub conscious and on and on

Across the continent
into your red heart
blue eyes and disintegrated mind....

Will the feel of your love ever leave me?
Gentle wind spirits around my lips.
My eyes open wide, open to my wild Irish mystic.
My button says, "Honorary Blarney Stone."

---

excerpt from "Irishman"

Your mother said you were a good lover and good
  with words.
So when you sent the winds to whisper in my ear,
When you asked the grasses to speak through my
  feet it captured me.
When I healed your spine holding you in my arms I
  was helpless.
You were my world for those months, and it was
  good.

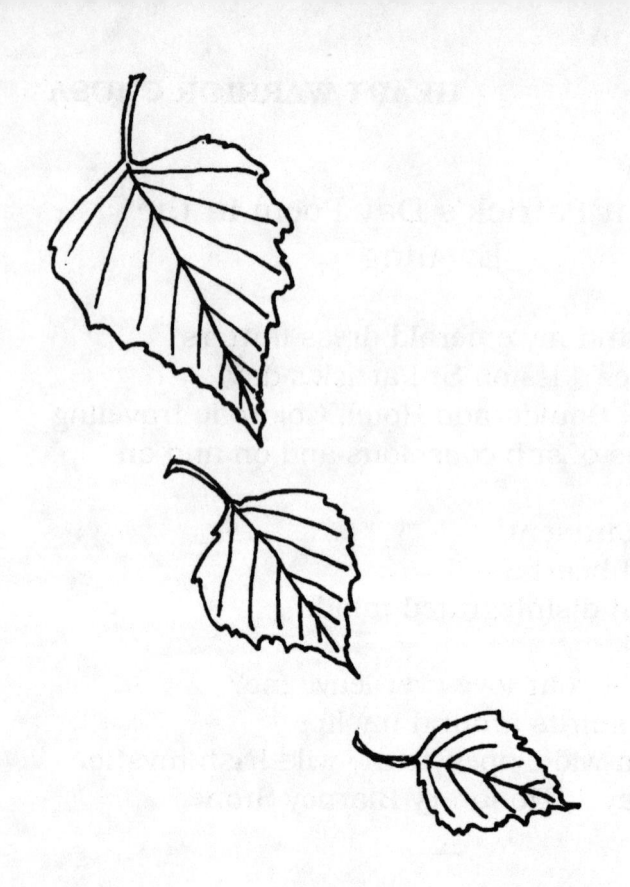

KARIN HOKKANEN

Birchtime

Birchtime is one of my favorite seasons of the year. After the long and snowy winter, then maybe an even longer chilly spring, the birches leaf out with green suddenness, confirming the promise of warmer days ahead. How wonderful to see that limey green light up the far shores of the lakes. How delightful to walk under a birch canopy on a lazy summer evening with friends.

In Finland, land of the birch-pine-spruce forests, the graceful *koivu* provided many of the necessities of life for the earlier people of the woods. The white bark, easily peeled from the trunks, is water proof and rot resistant and was used in roofing log homes under a layer of turf or wood shingles. Strips of bark were creatively woven into every imaginable product, from shoes and backpacks to knife sheaths and bowls. The underside of the bark is a beautiful shade of gold if collected before the midsummer and darkens to brown when collected later in the fall. During times of hardship, the birch could provide the materials for clothing, utensils, heating, and nourishment.

Birch leaves can be collected in the spring and used either fresh or dried to make a delightful and refreshing tea. The drink is a blood purifier, helping to clean out the toxins accumulated in the body over the winter. A tea made with birch, linden, and violets is a powerful cold remedy. Birch sap may be collected and drunk as a spring cure; the sap looks like water but has a wildly sweet flavor.

Birch branches, carefully collected and bundled together, are one of the main ingredients to the successful sauna ritual. The *vasta* or *vihta* is made from the ends of the wispy branches and is used the same day or set aside to dry for winter saunas. The birch whisk is soaked in a wooden bucket with water as the sauna is heated. To use the *vihta* while bathing, the wet switch is shaken over the sauna stones to give some steam, then gently used to beat arms, legs, and back with the leaves. Massaging tired muscles with the handle part is a treat for the body. The gentle thrashing leaves the skin clean and vibrant with a pleasant afterglow and aroma.

As you adventure in birchtime in the northwoods, take some long moments to enjoy the sweet scents and pleasures of the birch.

4 Untitled Poems

Hidden, the clouded stars
Conspire to stir
And swirl the constellations.
A wind, and the eye of the sky
Is opened.
Caught ashamed
They shiver into place.

Dawn stretches over two hours,
This morning, coldest of the year.
Smoke rises, then freezing falls—
Ten billion broken breaths
Glinting in the first edge of sun.

Silent trees lace the soft starless sky,
Patiently awaiting the wild wind
To give them voice.
Crystal-laden, the first breath
From the north
Teases them to whisper
The rumor of coming storm.

The night
Wrapped in the stillness of the rising fog
Explodes in the scent
Of a million shy blossoms
of spring.

Wildflower   Karin A. Hokkanen

KAIA DESHANE

You gave a Poem To Me
(for Becky)

You gave a poem to me when you
sheared that sheep
The way your biceps bulged
tiny woman with strong arms!
and patiently hitched up your glasses
framing intent eyes
twinkling as you called
a hundred wooly sheep
with marbley
eyes
by their
given names.

9 Mile Lake
(For Fred)

My hand gripped at the end of the warm paddle
is not separate from the wood—
I remember you made it—
I see a flock of ducks taking off noisily

then swiftly, quietly
all I hear
wings working.
This boat helps
when I can not swim.

KAIA DESHANE

One That Rhymes
(for Jesse)

Tansy, comfrey, chamomile, rue—
Look at what the herbs can do...
Yarrow, linden, cedar, pine—
We can be healthy
if we try!

Study and taste, pick and dry—
poultice, tincture, infusion, pie.
Under the dirt, under the sky,
peel the bark
pick the vine.

Boil the water, boil the root,
cleanse the blood,
soak the foot.
Touch the body, ask and find
what can help at the right time.

JANE WHITLEDGE

Pussywillows

One warm day
they fattened
in the grass—
flattened marsh

still patched
in snow: pussywillows
stroking the air.
They opened

long before the redwing's
return, its drill-
song and epaulets
commandeering spring.

Mittened harbingers,
the pussywillows
touched March softly,
came silently

as Braille. Then
as April snow fell
the pussywillows held
like snowflakes frozen

in the falling:
against that late snow,
each one exulting in
its fist of secret flowers.

(first published in *Yankee Magazine*)

Norwegian Maple — Karin A. Hokkanen

Contributors

Louis Bernard, a retired blacksmith, says that at age 82 he finds it harder to write his stories than tell them over a cup of coffee—homemade that is. He hopes to see the year 2001 so he can tell how it was in the 1900s.

Robert Beymer's heart and soul have resided in northern Minnesota since his first canoe trip as a Boy Scout in 1967. The rest of his body joined his heart and soul in 1984 when he and his wife, Cheryl, escaped from their urban life style and settled permanently in their home on the edge of the BWCA Wilderness. A former canoe trip guide, Robert is author of five guidebooks about the Quetico-Superior region.

Bob Cary is the dean of Ely writers. He became editor of the *Ely Echo* in its second year of operation and has continued with the *Echo* for more than twenty years. He is well known as an outdoorsman and has written five books about his fishing and camping experiences and the people that were part of his experiences. His latest book is *Tales of Jackpine Bob,* published by Pfeifer Hamilton.

Heart Warrior Chosa is a graduate of the Minneapolis College of Arts and has a MFA from Naropa Institute, Boulder Colorado. She has published several books and was a columnist for the *Ojibwe News.* Currently she is interested in "teaching children to harness their creative potential for story writing" using a child-sized Peter Pan set she designed. She is interested in trying the program with adults to "key them back into the imagination they knew as children."

John David moved from Baltimore, Maryland to Ely four years ago. He lives with a wife and three dogs on the Moose Lake Road. His wry humor and sense of irony make him a writer to take note of.

Kaia DeShane believes in simplicity and lives her life in a way that respects and does no harm to nature.

Dawn DeWitt is an urban center nurse transplanted to the northwoods. Her writing ideas are triggered by generational interaction and her interest is the interwoveness of generations. Her interests range from the written word to political cartooning.

Cathy Dybiec Holm, a freelance writer and musician living in Cook, Minnesota, enjoys writing creatively about the urban/rural connection and the interesting people she's met since moving from the Twin Cities to Cook two years ago.

Farrell is from Saint Paul, Minnesota but has lived near Ely for ten years. He writes comedy, for the stage, and "poetry that kind of slips out now and then."

Karin Hokkanen is sometimes referred to as a "Renaissance woman" because of her many interests: writing, gardening, books, bicycling, print making, historical crafts, medicinal plants and herbs. Many of her stories grow out of her experiences in living and travelling in northern Europe.

Becca Brin Manlove lives in the woods north of Ely. Her work reflects the details of her family and forest life.

Barbara Murray is a nontraditional student at Vermilion Community College in Ely and has just received her degree in Wilderness Management. She has been writing since she could put words together. Her work has ranged from the political to the personal. Currently she finds herself responding to and writing about the northwoods environment.

Lynn Rogers, "the bear man," is a wildlife biologist known worldwide for his black bear research and is the author of numerous scientific papers on bears. He is a cofounder of the North American Bear Center and Boundary Waters Ecology Center in Ely, Minnesota, and of The White Pine Society. He is a strong advocate for focused efforts to reestablish the white pine as a major part of the forest ecosystem from Maine through Minnesota.

Pauline Steffy taught English composition at the University of Alaska for seven years and worked as an editorial assistant and writer-editor. She has traveled extensively, is a Vietnam era veteran, an avid reader, and wife and mother. She has an enduring love of the English language and its ability to express emotion.

Anne Stewart lives in the northwoods and writes for a living. She has published several nonfiction books for middle school-aged children and writes for local and regional publications. She is currently working on a storybook for preschool children.

Margaret Sweet is a northern Minnesota native, born in Duluth and raised in Orr. She lived in Babbitt from 1958 until 1979 when she moved to Embarrass. In 1995 she returned to Babbitt. She has a long history in journalism which she has put aside at this time. She intends to continue her writing, interspersed with work, gardening, and reading. Margaret writes a monthly opinion column for the Duluth News Tribune and is working on two books: a collection of short stories about her cats and a biography of her mother.

Rose Thielbar learned to appreciate and enjoy the outdoors as a child growing up on a farm in Illinois. She has spent time in forty-eight states including Alaska and lived in Brazil, South America for five years. Her work experiences range from picking strawberries and raising cattle to writing for a newspaper and doing bookkeeping and income taxes. She married her high school sweetheart, and they raised three children together. Love of woods and water and the cool climate brought her to Minnesota's northwoods where she lives with all of the creatures who share this environment with her at the edge of the wilderness.

Margaret Vos: "Living in the home of my heart provides me the foundation for my work. I create what I love and love what I fashion, in beads, fibers, notes, words, and subtler media."

Jane Whitledge's poetry has appeared in *Yankee* and *Wilderness* magazines and numerous literary journals. She is currently working on completing a book collection of her poems.